Spirit
to
Run the Race

Spiritually Fit
to
Run the Race

A Personal Training
Manual for Godly Living

Kenneth C. Ulmer

A JANET THOMA BOOK

THOMAS NELSON PUBLISHERS®
Nashville

Published in Nashville, Tennessee, by Thomas Nelson, Inc.

Unless otherwise noted, Scripture quotations are from THE NEW KING JAMES VERSION. Copyright © 1979, 1980, 1982, Thomas Nelson, Inc., Publishers.

Scripture quotations noted NIV are from the HOLY BIBLE: NEW INTER-NATIONAL VERSION®. Copyright © 1973, 1978, 1984 by International Bible Society. Used by permission of Zondervan Publishing House. All rights reserved.

Library of Congress Cataloging-in-Publication Data

Ulmer, Kenneth C.
    Spiritually fit to run the race : a personal training manual for godly living / Kenneth C. Ulmer.
        p.   cm.
    Includes bibliographical references.
    ISBN 0-7852-7029-9 (pbk.)
    1. Christian life. I. Title.
BV4501.2.U46   1999
248.4—dc21

99-43089
CIP

Printed in the United States of America
4 5 6   04 03 02 01

Dedication

To my wife, Togetta,
the beat of my heart, the apple of my eye,
the wind beneath my wings

To my children, RoShaun, Kendan, Keniya, and Jody,
who make my heart glad

To the great people of the
Faithful Central Missionary Baptist Church, who graciously
allow me to fulfill my call and exercise my gifts

Contents

Acknowledgments

A work of this nature is never accomplished in the vacuum of solitude. With sincere gratitude and humble appreciation, I affirm and acknowledge those anointed, gifted men and women who contributed to the completion of this project.

This work grew out of the passionate seeds of a pastor's desire to equip the people of God for the work of the kingdom of God. My thanks to the flock of God who make up the Family of Faith, the Faithful Central Baptist Church where God continues to confront, challenge, and change me by the power of His Word. I praise God for your sincere hunger and thirst for righteousness.

I also praise God for the awesome staff He has given me—men and women who not only let their lights shine for the Master, but in whose light I am made to look good! Thank you for your encouragement, support, and for filling in the gaps in my ministry.

Thanks to Dr. Stan Gundry for planting the idea of transforming a series of teachings into the work presented here. Thank you for your big heart and honest advice.

I especially acknowledge and give God praise for my writing partner, Michelle Jones. I believe God has brought our lives together for such a time as this. Thank you for your insight, patience, and multi-faceted gifts. It is a joy to work with you as we work for the Master.

I thank God for my three children and my son-in-law. You

will never know how much your support means to me. Thank you for your prayers. Thank you for being proud of me. I am so very proud of all of you. Thank you for sharing me with the ministry. God has used you to make me what I am.

Finally, I give honor to my loving wife of almost twenty-five years. Thank you for allowing me extended times at the computer and for not embarrassing me when my mind continually wandered back to this project when it should have been on you and our time together. Thank you for distracting our son, Kendan, during those times when I probably should have been playing basketball or golf with him rather than polishing a chapter, page, or phrase. Your encouragement has been priceless as we serve God together. I am a better man because of you.

Part One
The Principle

Chapter 1
The Goal Is Godliness

Godliness is profitable for all things, having promise of the life that now is and of that which is to come.

1 Timothy 4:8

One of my life's passions is to be a good pastor, not just a good preacher or teacher—but a shepherd. Wherever you see the word *pastor* in Scripture, it translates as "shepherd." A good shepherd does more than just hang out with the sheep while they eat their fill of green pastures. A good shepherd guides his sheep. He coddles the weak ones and directs them to follow the stronger ones. He goes after the lost ones and binds up the broken ones. He protects his sheep from predators. A good shepherd loves his sheep.

I constantly look for ways to be more effective in fulfilling God's call for my life. My prayers to that end sound like a broken record, and my efforts keep me perpetually seeking. I read constantly, attend conferences, and study fellow pastors to glean whatever wisdom God would reveal. However, as zealous as I am to cultivate all available veins of spiritual education and enrichment, my mind settles on one elementary truth: the best how-to guides and role models for pastors are found in Holy Scriptures.

The Bible is a book after my own heart. It's the only book that completely satisfies me, because it's a book that can never be completely understood. The Bible is the only book on earth that can teach you what little you want to know, show you how much you don't know, and give you comfort and hope in your ignorance—all at the same time.

Recently, I sought the Lord's direction about where to focus my teaching for Faithful Central Missionary Baptist Church members, whom I pastor. I understood a new season was ahead, but beyond that, I wasn't sure what to expect.

At times my conversations with God sounded like outtakes from an Abbot and Costello comedy routine:

"Where am I, God?"

Where I put you.

"Where is that?"

I'll let you know.

"When?"

When I let you know.

This spiritual place has no windows and no doors but plenty of chairs. I choose one, sit in it, and wait. I make sure to sit, though, because I must be stabilized and centered just before He blows my mind . . . again.

I was casually reading 1 Timothy 4:6 when something caught my eye. Paul wrote, "If you instruct the brethren in these things, you will be a good minister of Jesus Christ." My study moved from casual to careful. Suddenly, I was captured by a basic spiritual concept that, surprisingly, was almost foreign to me. After I reread Paul's letters to Timothy and Titus, I discovered a recurring idea: godliness.

I have been saved for forty years; I accepted Christ as my personal Savior at the age of ten. I spent over fifteen years in postgraduate theological studies and have taught in both university and seminary settings. I have preached for twenty-two years and have been a pastor for seventeen of those years. I've preached hundreds of sermons and counseled hundreds of people for hundreds of hours. During that time and experience, I have never taught a lesson or preached a sermon on godliness, nor have I read a lesson or heard a sermon on it, taken a class on it, had a student ask a question about it, written or assigned a paper on it, or had a church member ask me about it. Yet, in 1 Timothy 4:7–8, Paul instructed Timothy to exercise or train himself "toward godliness" because "godliness is profitable for all things, having promise of the life that now is and of that which is to come."

Paul told us to train ourselves in godliness. Our target—the mark we shoot for, the purpose for which we are called—is godliness. The goal is godliness. Paul said teaching it would make Timothy a good minister, yet I had never taught one lesson on it. Godliness is profitable, or advantageous, in every situation, yet I have heard of only two books specifically written about it and have read only one of them completely. While I am by no means the definitive word on theological matters, I suggest that godliness, for all its importance, is possibly the least investigated, least researched, and least communicated discipline of the Christian life.

The Principle of Godliness

The word *godliness* appears fifteen times in Scripture, eleven of those in Paul's letters to Timothy and Titus. The remaining four occurrences are in 2 Peter. Godliness is by no means a purely Pauline concept, nor is it solely a New Testament phenomenon. On the contrary, the principle of godliness is present throughout the Scriptures.

Godliness in the Old Testament

In the Old Testament, godliness is implied in the summary of the lives of those saints who walked with God, had a heart for

Him, trusted in Him, and followed His ways. The closest term to godliness in the Old Testament is the Hebrew word *chasidh*, which means "kind, pious, or good" and is sometimes translated "saint" or "godly." It comes from a root word that means "to show oneself kind or merciful."

Another form of the word, *chesedh*, is often used to describe the loving-kindness or mercy that is central to the character of God. It's not clear if the people of God are called godly because they embody God's loving-kindness or because they are the object of it. Possibly both are true. Because they have received God's grace, godly people exhibit that grace in their own lives.

This Old Testament notion of godliness is rooted in deep faith or a reverential awe that expresses itself through obedience to God. It is interesting to note that in Psalm 16:10, *chasidh* is used to refer to the "Holy One" to come, or Jesus.

Godliness in the New Testament

In the New Testament, godliness is not implied or alluded to; rather, it is visible and obvious. The holy writers examined, exclaimed, and exhorted it. Jesus Christ, the sum and substance of all Scripture, embodied godliness. The New Testament word for godliness is translated from the Greek word *eusibius* meaning "devotion or piety toward God." It comes from two root words, *eu* meaning "well" and *sebomai* meaning "to worship." Together the words mean "a person falling back out of reverence or respect for someone great and lofty." To the Greeks, godliness was the fulfillment of obligations and resulted in acceptability to God.

In the Old Testament, reverence led to obedience. In the New Testament, the godly person structured his life around Jesus, living life as He lived it, and thereby revering and worshiping God.

The Components of Godliness

When you combine both the Old and New Testament concepts of godliness, their definition could be summarized as this: Godliness is consistent conduct that is consistent with the character of God. Let's explore this.

Godliness Results in Consistent Conduct

God is not just concerned with one-seventh of your life. Your Sunday-go-to-meetin' conduct, if it doesn't carry over into your Monday-through-Saturday conduct, does not impress Him. It's not how high you jump that counts; it's how straight you walk along the path once your feet return to the ground.

Consistent conduct is ongoing and unchanging. Godliness is continuous. The Scriptures are full of metaphors describing our relationship with God; few of them are static. Godliness is constantly moving. It cannot be turned on and off; it's always on. We run a race; we fight; we are sheep who graze and grow under the loving hand of our Shepherd. We are vines that bear fruit, and we are baby birds learning to fly. We are rich soil bringing forth the harvest of the Word.

Inherent in godliness is commitment. You have already made a commitment to God; otherwise, you could not pursue godliness. He has made one to you. Commitment by my definition means "you're in it for the long haul."

Godliness is also invariable. It is free from irregularity, permutation, or contradiction. What is godly today will be godly tomorrow. What is ungodly in one context can never be godly in another, regardless of the change in circumstances. This is not surprising when you consider the immutability of God. He created change, and yet He does not change, cannot change, and cannot be changed (James 1:17). He is God no matter where you are or what circumstances you're in.

While godliness is unchanging, Christians are not. Quite the contrary—we are always changing. If we required no changes, Calvary would have been in vain. The same would be said if we could not be changed.

Change is not a variable in the Christian walk, it is a given. But there is no fear in that fact. We already know what we will become. We are predestined to be conformed (changed) to the image of His Son (Rom. 8:29), who, like the Father, is the same yesterday, today, and forever.

Godliness Is Consistent with the Character of God

One of the most beautiful and complete earthly illustrations of our relationship with God can be seen in the loving dynamic between a father and son. As they walk together, one tiny hand secured by its giant counterpart, they tell the story. Junior walks with the confidence that there is nothing he can't handle because he's holding onto somebody bigger and "badder" than anybody or anything that could come his way. Daddy walks with the same assurance. He knows his son can handle anything because he's holding onto him. Did you catch that? Junior isn't worried because he's holding onto Daddy; Daddy's not worried because he's holding onto Junior. This is the picture of faith.

Every once in awhile you'll see a boy with his parents at the mall or some other place. The boy is cutting up and getting into things, and his mother has to repeatedly tell him to quit hanging from the display or stop running up the down escalator. This goes on for about ten or fifteen minutes before Mom looks at Dad in desperation. Then Dad merely says the boy's name. He doesn't even have to yell. Suddenly, the wild boy who was about to pull off the wig of a nearby mannequin is sitting quietly watching other wild boys whose daddies didn't come with them to the mall. This is the picture of obedience.

How do you get a young boy to obey? Command him? Any mother who's gone hoarse trying to get her son to take out the trash or clean up his room knows that's not the answer. Should you pay him? That only works when he wants something. The easiest way to get a boy to do something is to let him see his father do it.

Most boys want so much to be like their fathers that they'll study the way their dads walk, talk, and even how they hold their forks at dinner. In frustration, a mom may say to her son, "You act just like your daddy!" I'll let you in on a little secret: When you're not looking, your son will smile at that because that's exactly what he was trying to do! In essence, he worships his dad.

The common thread in all these illustrations is that both the motivation and the object of the behavior is the father. Likewise, the motivation and the object of godliness should be the Father in heaven. True godliness is consistent with the character of God. Here, consistent does not mean "ongoing or unchanging." Instead, it refers to a state of agreement or harmony with a person or principle, being in step with it; this does not mean we are equal to God in every way. For instance, God is omniscient, yet we are not.

But agreement with God should be evident in our behavior. For example, if we believe God knows everything, we shouldn't try to hide anything from Him. If we believe God is a jealous God, we shouldn't be unfaithful to Him. If God is all-powerful, we shouldn't try to fight Him. If He's truth, we should believe Him. If He's our Master, we should obey Him. If He's God, we should worship Him.

Godliness Begins with God's Revelation

Our definition of godliness—consistent conduct that is consistent with the character of God—carries with it the assumption that the godly person has some idea or understanding of the character of God. This is important and intentional. Godliness begins with the revelation of God through His Word and His Son by the power of His Holy Spirit.

As we progressively understand God's revelation to us, we become more godly. We change on the inside, and this then becomes apparent on the outside. Change should come as a natural outgrowth of immersing ourselves in God's revelation to us. Jesus' harshest criticism against the Pharisees was for godly behavior without the transforming power of God's love. He called them "whitewashed tombs which indeed appear beautiful outwardly, but inside are full of dead men's bones" (Matt. 23:27).

Most Christians have no real understanding of godliness because they have never been taught. They understand going to church and ministering to others. Some understand doing good deeds and helping people. Some understand doing spiritual things like reading the Bible and praying. But in all of this doing, they have not grasped godliness as a means or an end. If godliness is God's goal for our lives, then falling short of it is not an option. Yet, so much of our godly practice is, at best, good intention and, at worst, self-delusion.

In Chapter 2 we will clarify the concept of godliness by looking at some terms we often mistake for godliness and identifying the differences.

Then in Part Two, we will examine the process of attaining godliness, answering questions such as: *Where do I begin?* (Chapter 3), *How do I access godliness?* (Chapter 4), and *What exactly does God expect in regard to godliness?* (Chapters 4 and 5). We will also contrast godliness with sin (Chapter 6) and with counterfeit godliness (Chapter 7).

Finally, in Part Three, we will see what godliness looks like as it is lived out, focusing on the role of the Holy Spirit (Chapter 8), progressing toward maturity (Chapter 9), lessons from Christ's life (Chapter 10), and learning contentment (Chapter 11).

I do not want you to walk away from this book with nothing more than a new way to behave, though. Carrying a bigger Bible, putting a bigger fish on the back of your car, and hollering a little louder during praise and worship may get you seen, but it won't get you any closer to God.

Don't strive to be visible in the kingdom, but instead strive to be valuable. Ironically, when you do this, God will move heaven and earth to make you visible.

Prayer for Godliness

Father, bless me, Your child, with a thirst for
    godliness.
I reject a thirst for religion and a thirst for
    traditional spirituality.
I pray that I will become the man or woman of
    God You want me to be.
I desire to love You with all of my heart, mind,
    soul, and strength.
Finally, I pray with my brothers and sisters in
    Christ that we will become Your godly
    Church.
Bless us with an attitude of godliness.
Be the center of our focus, the focus of our
    faith.
In Jesus' name, Amen.

Chapter 1 Exercises

Exercise 1: Godliness Is Profitable for All Things

1. Memorize 1 Timothy 4:8: "For bodily exercise profits a little, but godliness is profitable for all things, having promise of the life that now is and of that which is to come."

Now look at 1 Timothy 4:8 as a collection of parts:

- Bodily exercise profits a little: Physical exercise is valuable for a little time.

- Godliness is profitable for all things: Godliness is valuable always for everything.

- Having promise of the life that now is: There is a reward for godliness here on earth.

- That which is to come: There is a reward for godliness in eternity.

Concentrate on each part until you understand it as completely as you can.

2. Read the following passages to add to your understanding of 1 Timothy 4:8. Write down any insights the Lord gives you.

- Psalm 37:5–11
- Matthew 6:33
- Colossians 3:1–4
- Romans 8:28

3. Memorize our thumbnail definition of godliness:

Godliness is consistent conduct that is consistent with the character of God.

4. Consider the main component of godliness—consistent conduct that is consistent with the character of God, which is behavior that is not only ongoing, but unchanging. Godliness is not an event, but a lifestyle. Moreover, it is not variable. What was godly yesterday is godly today. If it is to be considered godly, it must be in agreement with who God is. This does not mean we are equal to God. The Bible says beside God there is none other. Godliness is knowing the character of God and conducting ourselves in light of that knowledge.

Exercise 2: The Value of Godliness

Most would agree that godliness is a good thing. However, how many of us believe in the inherent value of godliness? The goodness of something speaks to its content—apart from us. The value of something speaks to how we embrace it and incorporate it into our lives. First Timothy 4:8 tells us that godliness is "profitable," which is to say it is valuable. A Christian cannot sincerely agree with that and then live an ungodly lifestyle. Take a look at the following examples of godliness from Scripture. What made these people godly, and how was godliness valuable to them?

Abraham—Genesis 22:1–18; James 2:21–23

_____

_____

_____

_____

_____

Noah—Genesis 6:8–18, 7:23, 9:1; Hebrews 11:7

_____

_____

_____

_____

_____

Mary of Bethany—Matthew 26:6–13; Luke 10:38–42; John 12:3

_____

_____

_____

_____

You—Psalm 37:23–24; Luke 6:43

_____

_____

_____

_____

You may find it difficult, at this point, to write in the space provided. It's easy to feel unworthy among people like Abraham, Noah, and Mary. But keep a few things in mind. First, the Bible tells us that all have sinned. *Godliness is not perfection.* You'll read that many times in this book. Also consider the fact that seeking God's will and direction is in itself a godly act. The more you seek God's righteousness, the more visible your own unrighteousness becomes. Don't lose heart. God only shines light on negative areas in your life that you're strong enough to face and He's strong enough to correct. If, on the other hand, you're running out of space extolling your own virtues, you might want to ask the Holy Spirit to do a little pride check.

Exercise 3: Consistent with Him

Godliness speaks of our harmonious interaction with God. He is God alone; therefore, no others come before Him. We are humble in the face of His greatness. He is gracious and loving, so we are grateful. He is clothed in majesty and honor, so we praise Him. Who we are can never be fully understood or realized without first knowing Him. It seems obvious, but most of us must learn that godliness begins with God.

Look at the following statements about God and determine, from their depiction of God, who you are expected to be by completing the sentence:

- The Lord is my shepherd, therefore . . .

_____

_____

_____

- There is nothing too hard for God, therefore . . .

_____

_____

_____

- The Holy Spirit teaches all things, therefore . . .

_____

_____

_____

- Jesus Christ died on the cross for my sins, therefore . . .

_____

_____

_____

Chapter 2
Not Quite Godliness

... Having a form of godliness ...

2 Timothy 3:5

While I was in Palo Alto, California, speaking at a conference and meditating on this book, my attention was captured by an interview on CBS's *This Morning*. Mark McEwen was interviewing actor Eddie Murphy about his newly released movie *Holy Man*. I had not seen the movie. In light of the anticipated irreverent perspective and its pseudo-sacred title, I was not interested in seeing it either. However, since I began writing this book, I have become more sensitive to any direct or indirect reference to any godliness-related statements, issues, or discussions.

My ears perked up when I heard the interviewer suggest that Murphy's career had suffered a slump, implying that his recent success was a kind of comeback. After a few brief statements about Eddie Murphy being the third highest-grossing actor in films, McEwen asked him, in a possible double-entendre reference to the *Holy Man* project, whether it had been difficult to maintain his spirituality during the highs and lows of his career. Murphy replied, "I've always been spiritually grounded."

I know absolutely nothing about Eddie Murphy's religious or spiritual life. However, I thought it was quite interesting that he characterized himself as "spiritually grounded."

Later McEwen asked Murphy how he regarded critics, entertainment writers, and the current climate of the entertainment industry. Murphy surprised me by saying that he doesn't read the newspaper. In fact, he said he hasn't read a newspaper for about three years. He said he gets his news through an occasional visit to CNN but mostly from observing what is going on in the world around him.

His next statement really caught me off guard: "The only way to know what's going on is to read the Bible." Murphy said he goes to the Bible to get an understanding of what is really going on in the world!

Now, this was by no means the first time a celebrity has used religious language. Eddie Murphy's use of the term *spiritually grounded* was not a surprise in and of itself. The thing that got me was that when he said it, I was keenly aware that I didn't really know what he meant. A little more light was shed on the scene when he referred to the Bible as his source for sociological analysis. However, since so many people regard the Bible as a generically inspirational book, which can be valuable without any significant allegiance to, submission to, or acceptance of its Divine Author, I am not always sure how highly they regard God's Word.

I am greatly concerned that some words, terms, concepts, and ideas that once had rather clear implications and interpretations have degenerated into contemporary clichés—the essence of which is often up for grabs. What does it really mean to be a spiritually grounded person? Does being spiritual mean that a person is godly?

Terms That Get Confused with Godliness

Our society has freely interchanged the concepts of religion, spirituality, holiness, and godliness. Such a casual switching back and forth of ideas may not only be inaccurate, but may even be potentially dangerous to the sincere seeker of God's will and His required way of life.

One of the challenges we face when considering spiritual issues is the fact that our pluralistic society has diluted, merged, synthesized, and made synonymous several terms. Because of society's attempts to be inclusive, we have virtually lost a historical understanding of these terms. Even churches have produced a set of clichés that contribute to misunderstanding. For example, "Praise the Lord" began as a call to worship, an exclamation of adoration. In many camps it has devolved into a mechanical greeting much like "Good morning" or "How are things going?"

Today's church lingo blends such terms as *religious, spiritual, holy,* and *godly.* Let's take a closer look at some of the nuances and connotations of these terms. What does it mean to be a religious person? What is spirituality? What does it mean to be a holy man or a holy woman? Finally, what is godliness?

Religiosity

What defines a religious person? What does it take to be religious?

To be religious is to be devoted to a religion. "Religion for many people connotes an established system and institution."[1] A person is called religious if he or she is committed to a set of theological principles or a certain philosophy. The religion's structure may be highly sophisticated or organizationally simplistic. It may be a given set of rules for life passed down through the ages as highly intricate and often complicated written literature, fully understood by only a few, but passed on to the masses of its constituency. Or, it may be an equally valid series of narratives woven into the very fabric of a given society by generations of storytellers.

Ironically, being called religious has an air of negativity in some camps. A religious person is viewed by many as old-fashioned, out of date, and out of touch with the reality of our contemporary society. Being characterized as religious is not always a compliment, as Eric Carlton noted in his book *Patterns of Belief: People and Religion:*

> Many people assume that traditional religion is out of date and cannot offer us wisdom for today. Religion in the . . . popular mind is still that other thing, that thing with doors and windows, clergy and tax-exempt status, moral expectations and social implications.[2]

As I write this section, I just heard a speaker on a news show refer to the "religious right." Again, this term has a negative connotation, an intimation of a philosophical and often political position of conservatism, even ultraconservatism.

This cloud of negativity is the result of a watering down of terms like *religion* and *theology.* Author Philip Sheldrake has also noted this trend:

> The word theology is now quite regularly used outside as well as inside religious circles to indicate a fiddling concern with any kind of irrelevant or unverifiable detail. As a result of such negative perceptions, there is a great deal of "practical Unitarianism" around these days. By that I mean that modern religious sensibilities are often content with a fairly undefined "God" and with Jesus as a great spiritual and moral teacher. If there is a sense of God's Spirit operating within time and space, it is likely to be confined to a kind of pantheistic understanding of the spiritual qualities of the earth or of matter generally.[3]

A lack of clarity and consensus in such terms as theology and religion is a reflection of our society's lack of clarity, and therefore, our lack of understanding of God, god, or gods. Our pluralistic generation seeks to be as inclusive as possible; this trend has spread to the church.

The scary thing about religion is that it looks like godliness to the carnal eye. It appears to love God with all its heart. It shouts on Sunday and goes to Bible study on Wednesday. Religion sings in the choir and knows more Scripture than the preacher. Religion visits the sick, volunteers at the mission, tithes, teaches, and disciples. Religion can be a deacon, usher, youth leader, or even a pastor. Religion is excited, motivated, busy, hardworking, and often the first to volunteer. So what's the problem? Religion's heart can be far from God. A heart that is far from God can never see God and, therefore, cannot know or exhibit true godliness.

In short, religiosity, is not godliness.

Spirituality

Spirituality is something that everybody seems to want these days. It is so sought after that it has become a contemporary buzzword. But no one seems to know exactly what it is. Nonetheless, they pursue it anyway. While many are quick to reject religion, the interest for things spiritual is seemingly at an all-time high. So, what does *spirituality* mean?

Difficult to define. At its most basic meaning, seeking spirituality is to hunger and thirst for things beyond the mundane—to, as Webster put it, seek things "of, relating to, consisting of, or affecting the spirit." No one would argue that to have spirituality is to be mindful of the things of the spirit. But this is where the definition gets muddy. What spirit should we be mindful of?

How does being mindful of spirit fit into religious beliefs, life philosophy, or just everyday living? You can see how the meaning quickly becomes elusive, and there are many reasons why.

Confusion of terms. One simple reason we are confused about the meaning of spirituality is because the word means many things to many people—from a purely secular, often nonreligious, and even unbiblical understanding to one that is rooted and grounded in the tenets of biblical faith. In his book *A Brief History of Christian Spirituality*, Bradley Holt noted,

> Spirituality—this ambiguous six-syllable term is new to many and objectionable to some. Although it is a clumsy word, it is used too much because it seems to do a task that no other word does. Religion for many people connotes an established system and institution, whereas "spirituality" implies personal involvement. "Spirituality" is a trans-religious word; it is not tied to one single faith.[4]

Sometimes the many diverse ideas of spirituality are not only unrelated to a single faith, but unrelated to any kind of faith at all. Some people think a person who sees a picture of the Virgin Mary in the side of the tree is spiritual. I know people who are into herbs and vegetarian diets. Some of their peers think of them as being somehow more spiritual than other meat-eating, toxin-contaminated consumers of preservatives.

Even the Church has been influenced by the lack of a solid definition for what is spiritual. When I was in South Africa a few years ago, a pastor friend told me about several South African indigenous churches where pastors often referred their parishioners to the local witch doctors for counseling. In fact, many pastors even patronized these witch doctors themselves for advice and blessings on how to grow their churches and develop a more effective ministry. In their eyes, going to witch doctors was the same as seeking spiritual counsel.

Much like jazz fusion, which takes a musical theme and adds variations on that theme until it is unrecognizable to anyone who tuned in during the middle of the piece, being spiritual today has become something quite removed from what it was in times past.

Change in theology. Another reason spirituality is difficult to define is because the source we have always gone to for its definition has changed.

In the past, spirituality for Christians and Jews was related to the God of the Bible, and people looked to the Church to set its definition: "spirituality [was] specific and [had] particular religious or doctrinal referents."[5] The definition of spirituality was closely and directly tied to the content of theology, which essentially means the study of what we know about God and how He works. Therefore, those who contemplated these things about God, meditated on them, and lived according to them would have been considered spiritual.

But that was when theology was a fixed entity. At one time we might have chosen to rest on the idea that our "theology was a stable body of knowledge, rich in the tradition of the past and secure enough to answer the questions of the present and the future."[6] We might have gone to bed each night with the assurance that all we believed was safely locked up in the vault of orthodoxy. Those days are gone.

Hans Urs von Balthasar, a Swiss theologian, made the same observation fifty years ago. Balthasar observed this rift "between theology and spirituality during the course of the past thousand years or so (at least in the West), and upon the devastating impact resulting from this growing divide for the life of all the churches."[7]

The only rule of present-day spirituality seems to be that there is no rule. There has been a disturbing progression about the concept of spirituality, drifting from being God-centered to being man-centered. If the spiritual life is man-centered, then the only criteria that matter are the ones that each man establishes for himself. God's standards of righteousness and life in the Spirit have been synthesized with humanism, compromised by "me-ism," and polarized from theism.

I can remember sitting in classes in seminary over twenty years ago, hearing my dispensational, conservative professors declare that you never judge the Bible by your experience; rather, you always judge your experience by the Bible. However, as Philip Sheldrake said in his book *Spirituality and History*: "in recent decades there has been a paradigm shift in the general approach to theology towards a greater reflection on human experience as an authentic source of divine revelation."[8]

Defining spirituality, then, is difficult if we base the definition on our theology because we live in an age of shifting theology, one that is anchored on shifting sand rather than the rock of God's truth. But such a weakening of theology is only evidence that the Church has not been vigilant in its role.

Carelessness of the Church. As I stated earlier, the Church originally defined the term *spirituality*. But over recent years we have done a poor job of setting the standard for spirituality in this world. My good friend Tony Evans said in his book *What a Way to Live!*:

The non-Christian society at large has failed to take the Person and Word of God seriously. And the church has been ineffective in its efforts to impact our culture for Christ at the deepest levels. Thus the church has contributed to the spiritual decline of American culture by failing to produce kingdom people who are accomplishing the kingdom agenda Jesus Christ laid down for us in the Word and by failing to clearly manifest and illustrate the solutions of the kingdom for the critical issues of our day. We have done an admirable job of cursing the darkness. But we have done a poor job of spreading the light.[9]

One of the reasons the world and seekers of spirituality have found it so difficult to clarify the concept of spirituality is because the Church has failed to clearly write the vision of true spirituality. Just as God instructed the prophet in Habakkuk 2:2 to write the revelation of the vision clearly, I believe God has mandated the Church to clearly publish God's idea of true spirituality. But lately we have not.

This is a point on which Satan has made great progress. We have been careless and neglectful, and the consequences have caught us unaware. Probably one of the greatest dangers of contemporary spirituality is that most of its disciples are oblivious to the fact that the spiritual dimension is the place of spiritual warfare. Satan exploits one's desire for the things of the spirit world by drawing the sincere seeker into the deceptive disguises of the demonic. Just as one of Satan's most common strategies is to convince us that he does not exist, another equally common, yet no less effective, ploy is to camouflage and disguise unrighteousness in the garb of righteousness. This is a real danger for the seeker who has not been grounded in the Word of God. It is also a wake-up call for those of us who know God's Word but fail to expose that deceit with the Truth.

Since spirituality, as we have seen, has become such a fuzzy, nonspecific, nebulous concept, we don't know what true spirituality is anymore. Moreover, if we could clearly define true spirituality, the master of disguise—Satan, our adversary—immediately moves to trick us and psyche us out! Tragically, the result is that even the most sincere seeker of God is often deceived into a state of pseudo-spiritual euphoria in a galaxy of the spiritual universe far, far away from both the Source of the universe and the True Light of the Son.

To help distinguish between products of Satan's deceit and the real thing, we will look closely at two of the most popular examples of counterfeit spirituality—New Age philosophy and self-help programs—and why they are not the real thing. Then we will clearly define what *is* the real thing—what true spirituality means.

Counterfeit Spirituality: New Age Movement

Possibly one of the closest things to a biblical concept of spirituality—yet still light-years away—is the New Age movement. I certainly don't mean to legitimize this movement by suggesting that it is biblical in essence. But I make this observation to emphasize the ability of this counterfeit movement to masquerade and appear to be biblical.

New Age is a "pseudo-everything." It is pseudo-religion. It is pseudo-spiritual. It is pseudo-theological. It has all the trappings of true spirituality, and its attempts to be universal, inclusive, and inoffensive have resulted in its being extremely attractive to the masses. However, New Age beliefs are far adrift from the moorings of biblical theology, spirituality, and religion.

Except for the obvious absence of direct references to Jesus Christ, New Age believers sound and look like real Christians. The New Age movement contradicts the duck principle—the one that says, "If it looks like a duck, walks like a duck, and quacks like a duck, it's probably a duck." New Age prayers may sound like the real thing. Its followers may walk without stress. Their language of love may sound like the real thing. But careful and closer investigation will reveal that New Age is, in fact, a camouflaged imposter of true biblical spirituality. Michael Downey made this point in his book *Understanding Christian Spirituality*:

> Some see in these trends a corruption of authentic spirituality. Many view New Age as a dabbling in the eclectic and esoteric. Not a few individuals and religious groups judge it to be a flagrant manifestation of the antichrist. But New Age is rather more a spiritual smorgasbord, a sort of salad bar approach to spirituality which invites a nibble here and there on whatever suits one's taste.[10]

I suspect that many in the New Age movement are products of, and maybe even members of, the true Church of the living God. Yet if you look closely, the New Age movement focuses almost solely on the spirit of man, not the Spirit of God. Its goal is to promote love, joy, peace, and harmony as it relates to the human spirit. In fact, New Agers believe that the human spirit is "divine" in itself—no need for the Holy Spirit of God.

The New Age movement has attracted all kinds of people— from ghetto gangsters who are fed up with the structure, irrelevant tirades, and impotent products of the traditional church, to celebrities who grace the radio airways, the pervasive intimacy of television, or the far-reaching influence of the silver screen. Spiritual seekers of all kinds—even Christians—find the New Age philosophy attractive. It seems to embrace all they are looking for.

However, a word of warning might be in order. If we are not careful, we run the risk of following after something that can actually take us tragically away from the true realm of the Spirit, which many of us seek. Our sincere search for the out-of-this-world experience, our hunger for something more, our craving for something deep can lead us into the very antithesis of that which we strive for. We may end up in a far country and think we have arrived home.

As a teenager I was the pianist for a youth choir in East St. Louis, Illinois. Angie (I've changed her name) was one of the prettiest and most popular girls in the choir and was often one of the featured soloists. She was also one of the most involved, participating in various youth activities of our small church.

Angie was brilliant, almost a straight-A student, in the National Honor Society, and a scholarship winner to several colleges and universities. I truly believe she was a child of God. I vaguely remember her being baptized, but I should say, I know now that going into the baptismal waters no more makes one a Christian than being parked in a garage makes one a car.

Upon graduation Angie went away to college. We stayed in touch with one another intermittently during college. Later, both of us moved to Los Angeles. At that time I was on the road back to the Father after spending much of my college life and military service in the far country of carnality. I was what the old folks back home used to call a backslider. I later learned that Angie was on a spiritual journey also.

After a rather tragic marriage, she had begun the work of putting her life back together. She went to several churches, trying to reestablish her relationship with God. She even joined a local gospel singing group and became one of its most faithful members.

Somewhere along the line, though, she heard a lecture on Transcendental Meditation (TM). Very early on in this new practice, she began to drift away from her more conventional spiritual affiliations—the church, the gospel group, and her circle of Christian friends. She acquired a new dimension of spirituality. She learned about mantra chanting. She became a disciple of the Maharishi. She not only attended Maharishi University and earned a doctorate, but also became a national instructor of that mystical Eastern discipline.

Many think Angie is a highly spiritual woman. She is a living testimony to the physical and psychological benefits of TM—lowered blood pressure, reduced stress, slowed aging process—and she gives lectures and scholarly presentations around the world. However, it seems that this newfound spirituality has, at best, marginalized her relationship with God to a relationship that shares the spiritual spotlight with the prophet Maharishi. At worst, the Maharishi has taken the central place of focus in her life. Jesus has become one of the prophets she respects but does not worship, not as she does the revered Maharishi.

Angie has attained her goal of a form of spirituality, but it has deceptively drawn her away from her God. Her story highlights the reality of Satan's deceptive exploitation of the sincere seeker of spirituality through presenting counterfeit spirituality as truth.

Counterfeit Spirituality: Self-help Programs

In surveying contemporary spirituality, one would be remiss to exclude the proliferation of self-help programs. The Twelve Steps of Alcoholics Anonymous have spawned a myriad of clones, imitations, and variations on that fundamental approach to deliverance from addiction. Perhaps the reason why this type of counterfeit spirituality is so powerful is that it produces good results.

Careful observation, however, reveals that these programs focus on a nebulous higher power, intentionally presented in a generic fashion to be pliable to fit one's personal definition of God or god (you choose). It is this reference to a higher power and the often life-changing, life-saving results that qualifies this as a legitimate form of contemporary spirituality. Yet the fact that the program is open to allowing the individual to define his or her own god is a focus that caters to the spirit of the human, putting the human being in charge.

The good news is that often through these programs the true and living God becomes the higher power of choice, in which case the results can be exciting.

I started my ministry career in music at a church in Los Angeles. My youth choir was a great bunch of teenagers, the Celestial Choir. Darlene was one of my strongest altos and was a most faithful member. After I left that church to concentrate on the ministry of the Word, I lost contact with her. Several years later, after becoming the pastor of The Family of Faith, where I now serve, I received a surprise request from Darlene for an appointment.

I was glad to see her but very amazed by the content of our conversation. She told me she was there because she was "working her steps." She had been on skid row in downtown Los Angeles, and God had pulled her out of her destructive rut. She said she had come to apologize to me for some of the things she had done to me.

I must admit I didn't even remember most of what she told me; however, it was a very tender moment to see this young lady struggling to get her life back together. What struck me most were her constant references to God and how she had turned her life over to Him again.

Darlene left that meeting, and I didn't see her again for several years. She showed up at a revival meeting where I was a guest speaker. The choir was composed of a large group of ex-junkies who had given their lives to Christ and were now ministering in the 'hood declaring the power of God to deliver people from the clutches of drug addiction. I was so very proud to see Darlene up there holding down the alto section—still singing about the glory and power of God.

Not long after that, Darlene attended The Family of Faith one Sunday and joined our church. As she came down the aisle at the end of service, I felt my eyes get heavy with tears. As I reached out to hug her, we both cried.

Today Darlene serves as a faithful member of the Voices of Faith, our adult choir, and she still holds down the alto section. I am so very proud of her. She is a product of a twelve-step program, proving that God can get His hand on people through such self-help programs. I praise God for bringing her back to church.

We must realize the danger of opening up vulnerable people to a nebulous higher power, or worse, by letting them create a god of their own choosing. We must not be naïve, since Satan can get quite a foothold if we provide a wide enough opening. People in crises form and develop a crucial life belief in choosing the god they will serve (or that will serve them). It is likely that such a belief, which will no doubt be seen as the rock that got them through the crisis, will then become a permanent part of their philosophy. For some, this will be a step toward the true and living God. For others, it will be the final nail in their spiritual coffin.

One great alternative is to adapt these programs according to the true God and His Word. Many churches, just as the one I pastor, have created such multiple-step programs to meet the needs of those struggling with addictive behavior. Our church has several success stories of people who have seen the power of God through these programs.

True Spirituality
The challenge we face in a quest for true spirituality is gaining a firm understanding of this concept. We must somehow

wade through the waves of humanistic commentaries and strain to plant the anchor of our faith in what God reveals and what God requires, even when it seems to contradict and conflict with the whims of men. This really is the dividing line—true spirituality is created by God, revealed by God, and is for the purpose of serving God. Man, to serve his purposes and pleasures, however, creates counterfeit spirituality.

The following characteristics will shed more light on what separates true spirituality from counterfeit.

True spirituality must be solidly rooted and grounded in the Word of God. Tony Evans has observed: "The Bible is not the Word of God emeritus. It's not a book that you throw by the wayside or put on the coffee table just to look good. It is the manual of authority in God's kingdom, the book from which our kingdom agenda is drawn."[11]

Yet it seems that the Bible has become, at best, a reference book for the very Church whose birth and agenda is established in it. It is no longer the ultimate source of doctrine, reproof, correction, or instruction in righteousness, which is God's definition of spirituality in 2 Timothy 3:16. Tony Evans tells it like it is: "Christians . . . want to switch books. They want to use the Bible when it's convenient, sort of like making God a servant in His own kingdom. But it won't work. The Bible must be the authority that governs every area of life."[12] God's revealed and written Word is not an optional extra. It is the mandate of the Master.

True spirituality includes a true relationship with God the Father, God the Son, and God the Holy Spirit. Attempts to be a good person or a "deep" person in one's own strength do not qualify for true biblical spirituality. Counterfeit spirituality often produces good people, people who are deep. However, to brand those persons as spiritual is a misuse of the term.

The focus of true spirituality is on the Person of God and His

Son. The focus is on the empowerment and enabling of the Holy Spirit. By contrast, the center of counterfeit spirituality is man. The Trinity provides all a person needs for spirituality: from God, authority and revelation; from Christ, an example; and from the Holy Spirit, power.

True spirituality results in a steadfast commitment to God's ministry. There is a tendency to try to draw closer to the Master without truly committing to His ministry. Kenneth Leech observed this in *The Eye of the Storm*:

> Bishop Charles Gore, writing in the early years of the twentieth century, commented that there was a tendency in protestantism towards a conception of spirituality that was certainly not completely Christian, one that dissociated the material and social dimensions of life from the realm of the spirit.[13]

The focus of counterfeit spirituality is inward in a so-called attempt to tap the power of God within. Such a seeker is content with simply that. However, through the lens of God's love, a true revelation of the living God will automatically refocus the true seeker on the needs of the world. He or she will be compelled to action directed by God's Word.

For all that can be good about true spirituality, it is impossible without godliness, and counterfeit spirituality is certainly nowhere near godliness.

Holiness

I was born and raised in East St. Louis, Illinois. Most kids in my neighborhood went to one of several churches within a six- or seven-block walking distance. When I was in the fifth grade, twin girls moved about three blocks from my house. They came to East St. Louis from somewhere in the South; I think it was Mississippi. From the first day these two girls came to school, the kids used to tease them and whisper about them behind their backs. The topic of conversation was their clothes—always long dresses, never pants or shorts. Even in junior high and high school when some girls began to wear makeup, I never saw either of them wearing the slightest bit of lipstick or eye shadow. They were attractive, and yet they were considered plain Janes.

You see, the twins were sanctified girls. They were members of a Holiness church that denounced makeup, dancing, card playing, short dresses, and women wearing pants. (Some other churches hold to these same beliefs as well.)

The long dress-wearing twins were my first exposure to holiness and sanctification. I had no idea of the theology or doctrine they believed in, but I was most impressed that they led a distinguishable lifestyle based on their religion, their church affiliation, and their relationship with God. Don't get me wrong—they were not unsociable loners. Although they did not attend some of the social activities in our circle—they didn't dance or go to the movies—they were very personable, fun-loving girls. Both of them had the cutest dimples and smiled all the time.

However, they were willing to suffer ridicule for their beliefs about God and their church. I often thought, if I were them, I would have either changed my wardrobe or hid some clothes in my book bag so I could change after I left home. I certainly didn't think I could have taken the teasing they endured. I know now that I am indebted to my neighborhood friends for giving one example of what it can mean to be sanctified and to live a holy lifestyle.

Much later in life, however, I learned that holiness is about much more than what kind of clothes you wear.

Defining Holiness

The word *holy*, in various forms, occurs more than six hundred times in the Bible. The third book of the Torah, the Pentateuch, is the book of Leviticus. The main topic of Leviticus is holiness.[14] Holiness for the believer is not a suggestion from God. We are commanded to be holy (Lev. 11:44). Like so many, my flawed understanding of holiness formed my opinions about the Mississippi twins. In *The Pursuit of Holiness*, Jerry Bridges warned against this error:

> In some circles, holiness is equated with a series of specific prohibitions—usually in such areas as smoking, drinking, and dancing. The list of prohibitions varies depending on the group. When we follow this approach to holiness we are in danger of becoming like the Pharisees with their endless lists of trivial do's and don'ts, and their self-righteous attitude. For others, holiness means a particular style of dress and mannerisms. And for still others, it means unattainable perfection, an idea that fosters either delusion or discouragement about one's sin.[15]

Holiness is one of those terms that we toss about in our more spiritual conversations, yet probably never really understand. Certainly, we would make some major adjustments in our lives and lifestyles if we had a handle on its true meaning. The famed Anglican evangelical John Stott spoke of our struggle with the concept of holiness in a message delivered at All Souls Church in London.

Dr. Stott said that we are more comfortable with the adjective *holy* than with the noun *holiness*. Stott said that we use terms like *Holy Communion, Holy Bible, holy matrimony, holy baptism, holy man*, and *holy woman*. However, holiness sounds sanctimonious. He observes that our unfamiliarity with this term may be a token of the degree to which we have drifted from a Christian mind to a secular mind.[16]

As a beginning point, we know that, on one level, holiness is all about God. The simple dictionary definition tells us what *holy* means: one who is "exalted or worthy of complete devotion as one perfect in goodness and righteousness." We know that only God fits that description to a tee.

It absolutely blows my mind when I ponder the concept of the holiness of God. The closer I get to Him, the more I see of Him, and the more I learn about Him, the more convinced I am that I am not like Him. Then I am reminded that God says I am to be holy just as He is holy. I am more and more reminded that I am trying to be like a God whom I don't really know at all.

At the heart of holiness is an element of mystery and of the unknown. Rudolf Otto, in his book *The Idea of the Holy*, called this mystery "the numinous." He uses this word in speaking of the divine holiness of God and says it ". . . has in it something of fear (the feeling of awe and danger that flows from knowing one is in God's hands for weal or woe), and that God is neither subservient nor tame," but fear wedded to fascination (the feeling of being allured, even entranced, by God's beauty, goodness, mercy, and love).[17] Otto draws attention to the fear, the wonder, the shock, the amazement, and the astonishment which the holy may evoke. The holy is *mysterium tremendum et fascinans*. It knocks us back and draws us on.[18]

On the one hand, we are drawn to the holiness of God, and on the other hand, we tend to run from it in the shame of our unworthiness and inadequacy to emulate that very holiness.

Sharing in the holiness of God means taking on His transferable attributes. God is omniscient, omnipresent, and omnipotent. He is the all-knowing, everywhere, all-powerful God. We will never share these incommunicable attributes. We will never know it all, although we might meet some who think they know it all! We will never be able to be in two places at one time, although we often plan our days and schedules as if we could. We will never be all-powerful. However, we can be holy as He is holy and like Him in his holiness.

But how is it possible to live up to such a calling?

Holiness: Our Position in Christ

Praise God, He doesn't leave us on our own for this one! Holiness has to do with our spiritual position in Christ. The Bible says we are saved by grace through faith (Eph. 2:8). This faith response to the love of God results in a person being placed in the body of Christ: "For by one Spirit we were all baptized into one body" (1 Cor. 12:13). The word *baptize* means "to immerse or submerge into an element." The idea is that the believer is baptized or identified spiritually into and with the body of Christ, the Church.

Fritz Rienecker and Cleon Rogers noted in *A Linguistic Key to the Greek New Testament*: "Paul is not referring to water baptism but to the spiritual transformation which puts the believer 'in Christ,' and which is the effect of receiving the gift of the Spirit which takes place at conversion."[19]

To be "in Christ" suggests a transportation—to be no longer in the world but spiritually transported into the body of Christ, to be no longer in sin but relocated into a saving relationship with Him. Salvation places us in a new position as it relates to God. As John Stott said,

In New Testament language somebody who is "in Christ" is a Christian . . . [the] preposition "in," when used in relation to Christ, is not used spatially. To be "in" Christ does not mean to be "inside" Christ, as the family is in the house when they spend an evening together, or as clothes are kept in a cupboard or tools in a box. No, to be "in" Christ is not to be located inside him or to be locked up in him for safety, but rather to be united to him in a very close personal relationship. Jesus himself put this beyond dispute by his allegory of the vine and the branches. "Abide in me, and I in you," he said to the twelve. "As the branch cannot bear fruit by itself unless it abides in the vine, neither can you, unless you abide in me. I am the vine, you are the branches. He who abides in me, and I in him, he it is that bears much fruit, for apart from me you can do nothing." It is evident from this metaphor that to be and to abide "in him" was to enjoy a living and growing relationship with him. *The Good News Bible* is quite correct to render the words "in Christ" by the expression "in union with Christ."[20]

Salvation also places us in a new position relative to Christ through transformation: "Therefore, if anyone is in Christ, he is a new creation; old things have passed away; behold all things have become new" (2 Cor. 5:17). It is this understanding of being in Christ that gives us insight into the concept of holiness.

In Colossians 1:27, Paul said the mystery of the gospel is "Christ in you, the hope of glory." Did you get that? Christ is in you. When you were saved, a marvelous mystery was manifested in you. Christ came to dwell in you. Where, before, God used to dwell in temples made by hand; He now dwells in His holy temple—you! The mystery of salvation is that, by the power of the Holy Ghost, the living Christ lives in us (1 Cor. 6:19). Wow! But now, before you shout all over the house, don't miss the dual dimensions of our salvation: Christ in you! You in Christ! This is a kind of reciprocal indwelling. Allow me to illustrate.

When I was a little boy, we used to go to Mississippi and

Alabama every other summer to visit relatives. My cousin Mattie lived way, way back in the country and had no central heat in her house, but she had fireplaces in several rooms.

One of the thrills we had as kids was to gather firewood and place it on the fire. You can tell we were from the city and didn't do this sort of thing on a regular basis. We actually thought it was fun. In order to keep the fire burning, every now and then Cousin Mattie would stir the fire with a poker. I noticed that if she left the poker in the fire for a long time, the tip would get red-hot and glow. One time, I pulled the red-hot poker out of the fire and accidentally touched some paper. Immediately the paper caught fire.

As I reflected on that incident, I realized that I had to put the poker in the fire to get the fire in the poker. The poker was in the fire; the fire was in the poker. Likewise, Christ is in you, and you are in Christ—a kind of reciprocal indwelling.

So where does holiness come in? Salvation relocates my life into Christ. God now sets me aside for His use and His use alone. I am sanctified and "holy-fied." A life of holiness is one lived with constant awareness. In fact, it is a life with an almost habitually subconscious awareness that you are God's man or God's woman. You have been called out from the ways of the world unto the things of God. You have been set aside from the world and kept for God's use alone. God has loved you into a position of holiness—a special, sacred relationship with the Almighty.

God loved me enough to place me on holy ground. I ought to love Him enough to live my life there—in holiness. Jonathan Edwards, in his book *Religious Affections*, put it this way:

A true love of God must commence with a delight in His holiness and not with a delight in any other attribute. Herein consists the beauty of saints, that they are saints or holy ones. The moral image of God in them is their beauty and their holiness. The Christian faith is beautiful above all other religions because it is so holy a religion.[21]

The challenge I face as a believer is to keep my eyes on God's holiness. Possibly no other attribute challenges and changes me more than a perpetual view toward the holiness of God. If I can focus my life on His holiness and the power He gives me there, I will find myself growing from glory to glory (2 Cor. 3:18).

The concept of holiness, however, is only part of our goal toward godliness.

Godliness: The Sum of the Parts

Religiosity, spirituality, and holiness are requirements in our Christian walk, but in and of themselves, they are not the whole. If you were to place each of those concepts over one another, the area of overlap would give you godliness. Consistent conduct, consistent with the character of God, is the sum of the obedience required by religiosity, the faith inherent in spirituality, and the worship that overflows in response to holiness. If each of these concepts is practiced separately as a substitute for godliness, this would be as dangerous to a believer as willful disobedience.

Religion by itself can be tempted to conclude, "I can do the things of God and be godly." But Jesus taught us to seek first the kingdom, and the feeling and the doing will be added to you. When godliness influences religion, religion becomes humble. As a result, we see the Church produce selfless good works motivated by God's grace.

Spirituality alone can be tempted to conclude, "I can desire the things of God and be godly." But a powerful Christian walk takes spirituality combined with godliness to make the connection between desire for the things of God to mindfulness, commitment, and action toward the things of God.

Holiness can be tempted to conclude, "I can look like the things of God and be godly." But when holiness is influenced by godliness, a person becomes aware of his position in Christ, which overflows into worship and a lifestyle that naturally sets him apart.

Godliness puts God in the center of all our efforts toward eternity. With that done in those efforts, godliness becomes our sufficiency. It is faith, hope, and charity. It is the expression of the Father, the example of the Son, and the exhibition of the Holy Spirit. Godliness is valuable in this life and the life to come. It is God's goal for us.

The Pathway to Godliness

My goal for you, my deepest desire for you, is that you would be a godly woman or man. My deepest desire for my children is not that they find a good career and make money, but that they become men and women of God. Some of you are looking for loving, intimate relationships. In that seeking remember to look for a person who loves the Lord.

Your desire should be that all your relationships reflect godliness, so that you can be a light to the world. I am talking about a real, practical, day-to-day, rubber-meets-the-road, nitty-gritty godliness that is perceptible in your everyday life. This kind of godliness rubs off on those who get too close to you. My desire for you is that your goal in life would be godliness. The Bible says a church that is filled with godly people will grow and will know the comfort, the presence, and the power of the Holy Spirit.

In Part One, we have attempted to give you a basic definition of godliness—what it is and what it is not. In Part Two, we will explore the process of attaining godliness—where it begins, how to access it, and exactly what God expects from us.

Prayer
for
Holiness

Heavenly Father, I thank You for receiving me
    as Your child.
I thank You for my holy position in Christ.
Thank You for the ministry of Your Holy Spirit
    that empowers me to walk in holiness.
Father, I pray that I might not slip into the
    routine of ritualistic religion or fall prey to
    counterfeit spirituality.
Help me to be ever mindful of the subtle
    imitations of true godliness that infest
    this world.
Give me wisdom and discernment so that I may
    live my life in a manner that truly
    represents Your holiness.
Lord, give me a hunger and thirst for Your
    righteousness.
Father, I desire above all to be holy, as You
    are holy.
Grant it, O Lord, in Your mighty name. Amen.

Chapter 2 Exercises

Exercise 1: A Complete Package

1. Memorize 1 Thessalonians 4:7: "For God did not call us to uncleanness, but in holiness."

Godliness is the intersection of religiosity, spirituality, and holiness—the place where all three meet. Each of these things alone is not enough to encompass the whole of godliness. One cannot be godly unless his conduct encompasses all three. While the three examples in Chapter 1's exercises gave us a picture of godliness, each emphasized a different aspect of it. The testing of Abraham is an exceptional illustration of the faith required by spirituality. Noah shows us the obedience required by religiosity. And Mary of Bethany is a portrait of the worship inherent in holiness.

Faith, obedience, and worship are respectively the essence of spirituality, religiosity, and holiness. They are the behavioral components of godliness. They are what we do as we go toward godliness. As spirituality, religiosity, and holiness are connected, so are faith, obedience, and worship. But each of the latter is interdependent. Faith, obedience, and worship must operate together, or they cannot operate at all. It's important to understand this if we are to understand godliness. Many of us are unfulfilled and impotent in our Christian walk. This is not because we don't believe, but because our belief is nullified by disobedience. Or, perhaps, if we do obey, we do it for our own glory because we have not incorporated worship into our lifestyle.

2. Study the following equations, then consider them in light of the examples given from Scripture. Try to match the example

to the correct equation. As you complete this exercise, look at your own life. Think about how faith, obedience, and worship are exhibited in your behavior and your relationships.

Complete Equation:
Faith + Obedience + Worship = Godliness in Action

Incomplete Equations:
Faith - obedience = Dead faith
Faith - worship = Misdirected faith
Obedience - faith = Self-serving obedience
Obedience - worship = Self-centered obedience
Worship - faith = Insincere worship
Worship - obedience = Incomplete worship

Matching

Dead faith	Saul
Misdirected faith	Pharisees
Self-serving obedience	The children of Israel
Self-centered obedience	Jonah
Insincere worship	The rich young ruler
Incomplete worship	Samson

Answers:
- *Dead faith: Jonah* believed God had spoken to him, but his belief was nullified by his disobedience (Jonah 1:1–2:10). Interestingly, Jesus uses the example of Jonah to illustrate his own death.
- *Misdirected faith: Samson's* faith was without reverence for the God who had given him his strength, so he looked to himself for his deliverance once too often (Judg. 13:1–16:20).
- *Self-serving obedience: The rich young ruler* was obedient,

but he did not believe Jesus enough to give up all he owned (Mark 10:17–25).

- *Self-centered obedience: The Pharisees* were obedient, but they believed it was their obedience that made them righteous. So, they became self-righteous (Matt. 12:1–14).
- *Insincere worship: The children of Israel* worshipped God, but their unbelief kept them out of the Promised Land (Heb. 3:7–12).
- *Incomplete worship: Saul* tried to worship the Lord, but he did this only in an effort to cover his disobedience. It cost him his throne (1 Sam. 15:1–23).

Do any of these examples of incomplete godliness ring true in your life? If we're honest, all of us can find ourselves somewhere in this exercise.

Exercise 2: Focusing on God

Part 1: God is so focused on us, watching our every move, never sleeping, protective, loving, gentle, and merciful. We are precious to Him. What if He were that precious to us? What if we purposed to know Him, care for His needs, and make Him precious?

Get alone. Turn off the phone. Shut out as much noise as you can. Be very still. Imagine that you have God's undivided attention, because you do. Think about how precious He is to you. Speak to Him with your thoughts. If you can't think of anything, consider Him as Father. What is it about your Dad in heaven that makes you proud to be His child? In what ways are you glad to be like Him? How do you want to be more like Him? Try to spend at least fifteen minutes with this. Your mind may wander. As soon as you're aware of it, bring your focus back to God by thinking, *Forgive me for wandering, Lord. You're precious to me because you're* . . . (fill in one of God's attributes).

Part 2: Stop speaking and listen. Try to deliberately silence every mental effort on your part. What are the things that come to your mind? Are there images of God or Scriptures or songs? Does this process bring up thoughts about you? Whatever it is, jot it down in the margins of this page or in a journal. It may be difficult, at first, to discern which thoughts are yours and which ones are the Holy Spirit speaking to you. If you're not sure, write your thoughts down. Again, try to spend at least fifteen minutes with this.

Part 3: Pray with your heart. Pray aloud so you can focus on what you're praying. The Lord may have given you something to pray about. If you're not sure how to start, begin by using the prayer provided on page 43. Don't forget to thank Him.

Part
Two

The Process

Chapter 3

Fear: The Beginning of Godliness

Work out your own salvation with fear and trembling.
Philippians 2:12

A couple of years ago, I traveled to England to complete a series of courses in theology at Oxford University. At the time, the local papers were covering the story of a West London community in a painful uproar over the rape of a nine-year-old girl. Perhaps as tragic and astonishing as the crime was, the fact that the crime was committed at lunchtime by five schoolboys—four ten-year-olds and one nine-year-old—made it even worse. Forty years of walking with God and all my units of ecclesiastical education and countless hours of prayer and meditation had not prepared me to handle this tragedy with any greater degree of composure or detachment. In fact, I have found that over the years, my heart-level reactions have become amplified. If I was once confused by random acts of cruelty, I am now confounded. If I was once broken, I am now shattered inside when faced with the almost gleeful destruction of human life.

Most disheartening to me, though, was the attitude of the community mirrored in the responses of some of the parents whose children attended school with the preteen rapists. One parent said the heinous incident was the fault of the school administration for not providing enough security. Another blamed the girl's teacher for not being more attentive to her students. Related to that was the suggestion that the teachers restore discipline in the schools. Yet another parent said the police should have been better at patrolling what they knew was a crime-infested neighborhood. No one said it was the fault of the five boys or their parents. The problem was not a lack of security from school administration, supervision, discipline by teachers, or patrolling by police. The problem was a lack of fear in those boys and the failure on the part of their parents to instill that fear.

When a child is born, the first order of business is to establish in him an understanding of the sufficiency and authority of his parents. Sufficiency is the basis for growth. If a child understands that he is not alone and that his needs are taken care of, he becomes increasingly more secure and independent, which encourages him to explore and expand his physical, mental, and emotional base. Most parents don't have a problem with providing that. Even as adults, growth is primarily a function of one's perceived security or need for the same.

Establishing authority is another thing altogether. If sufficiency is the seed of growth, authority is the seed of direction and self-control. Sufficiency encourages a child to walk. Authority encourages a child to walk straight. Sufficiency is grounded in need. Authority is grounded in fear, which is why it is sometimes a difficult proposition. We are uncomfortable with the idea of being feared, especially by our kids. But a rule that cannot or will not be exercised is meaningless. Laws that carry no threat of punishment are little more than suggestions. And boundaries are only effective if there are consequences attached to breaching them.

It is no accident that God's relationship with us is often described in parental terms. Like any good parent, the Father establishes His sufficiency by responding to our needs. However, sufficiency alone is inadequate to ensure the safe, healthy development of His offspring. If we are driven solely by our needs, then Satan can and will provide any number of alternate sources to meet those needs, every one of them guaranteed to move us further away from God.

Authority, on the other hand, is singular by nature. Certainly, there are many sources of influence in our lives, but ultimately only one authority. If you're wondering who or what the authority is in your life, ask yourself whom or what you're most afraid of denying or disappointing. For some it is a parent, for others a spouse. Your children could be the authority in your life, or maybe it's your boss. Some people are their own authority. Dictators and serial killers are an extreme outgrowth of this mindset. For the man or woman who would be godly, however, there can only be one Authority, and He is God. He is the One we should fear rejecting or offending above all others. You cannot be a godly man or woman and not fear God.

A Two-Sided Coin

We learned in the first chapter that reverence for God is the very essence of godliness as translated from the Greek word *eusibius*. Not surprisingly, that reverence finds its foundation in the concept of fear. Fear, as revealed in Scripture, is a complex concept. A complete understanding of godly fear requires examination beyond contemporary theological sources, since during the past thirty years, writers have only emphasized one aspect of it.

The most common interpretation of the word *fear* is that it is the legitimate acknowledgment of the greatness of God. To reverence God means to "hold Him in high esteem, to have a wholesome, holy respect for God." It is to affirm the "wholly otherness" of God, to declare Him in a category all by Himself. I hold God in the highest place of honor in my life. He is Number One, and my ultimate goal is to please and give homage to Him. This positive connotation of fear is popular with today's scholars and commentators, possibly due to the touchy-feely-everything-is-beautiful influence of the sixties. However, a complete understanding of fear goes beyond that.

Think of fear as a two-sided coin. One side means "reverent fear." When you flip the coin over, the same word means "to be afraid of God." To fear God means . . . to fear God, to be afraid of Him. Don't back away from that. It's not deep. It's not a figure of speech. Take it at face value. This very sentence doesn't sit well with many of us. We struggle with this because it raises questions that force us to see a side of God we're not always comfortable with. Why does God want us to be afraid of Him? How can a God of love want His children to be afraid of Him? Perhaps some clarity can be found in extending our coin metaphor.

Look at the sides of the fear coin as Truth and Consequences. One side is reverence, the result when the truth of God is revealed to us. The other side is holy "afraid-ness," the result of the potential consequences of violating that truth. You see, there is a progression within fear. Simply put, my fear or reverence of God makes me scared of Him. Once I realize that He is omnipotent, I develop a wholesome fear of His power. Once I realize He is omniscient, I should have a healthy fear of any attempt to deceive Him or keep something from Him. Once I realize that He is omnipresent, I have a fearsome concern for my actions, no matter where I am. Once I realize that He is really God, fearing Him means I take Him seriously.

Now, our discomfort is usually heightened at this juncture because we know we're not afraid of anything unless we believe it can hurt us. How, then, does this jibe with our picture of the

Lord, our Shepherd, our Refuge, the Caretaker of the vineyard? Would He hurt us? Let me ask you some questions. When a child misbehaves, do you punish that child? How do you punish him? Do you tickle him, or buy him a bike? Of course you don't. You want the pain of the punishment to correct the misbehavior. Hebrews 12:5–6 exhorts us, "Do not despise the chastening of the LORD, nor be discouraged when you are rebuked by Him, for whom the LORD loves, He chastens." A good parent disciplines his or her child. Will God discipline us? Yes. Will it hurt? Sometimes. But consider the alternative put forth in Hebrews 12:8: "If you are without chastening, of which all have become partakers, then you are illegitimate and not sons." If you're acting up and God's not disciplining you, you'd better check to see if you're His child, because parents only discipline their own children. As believers, we don't live in fear of God's judgment. But we should be very concerned with the correcting rod of His discipline.

If you're uncomfortable with the truth-and-consequences portrait of fear, consider a more biblical-sounding, though no less striking, image. Using our coin again, think of one side as God's grace and the other as His mercy. Grace is when God gives you what you don't deserve. Mercy is what God gives you when He doesn't give you what you do deserve.

We show reverence for God when we realize how holy, high, mighty, and magnificent He is, and we wonder why He'd even bother with little ol' lowly us. This represents His grace. We're afraid when we realize that all have sinned. Because all have sinned, we have sinned. The wages of sin is death, so God could've killed us. But we're not dead. This represents God's mercy.

O Lord, I am astonished at the difference
between my receivings and my deservings,

between the state I am now and my past gracelessness,
between the heaven I am bound for and the hell I merit.
Who made me to differ, but thee?
for I was no more ready to receive Christ than were others;
I could not have begun to love thee hadst thou not first
loved me,
or been willing unless thou hadst first made me so.
O that such a crown should fit the head of such a sinner!
such high advancement be for an unfruitful person!
such joys for so vile a rebel!
Infinite wisdom cast the design of salvation
into the mould of purchase and freedom;
Let wrath deserved be written on the door of hell,
But the free gift of grace on the gate of heaven.[1]

The Path of Fear

Godliness by definition includes a holy fear of the Lord. It is that fear that sets a godly man or woman on the path to knowing God's will for them and pulls them back to that same path when they stray. Job said, "Behold, the fear of the Lord, that is wisdom, / And to depart from evil is understanding" (Job 28:28). David said, "The fear of the LORD is the beginning of wisdom; / A good understanding have all those who do His commandments" (Ps. 111:10). Solomon echoed his father's sentiments with "The fear of the LORD is the beginning of knowledge, / But fools despise wisdom and instruction" (Prov. 1:7). The fear of God is where true wisdom begins. In other words, the first thing a smart person learns to do is fear God. Where there is no fear of God, there will never be godliness. A person who doesn't respect the person of God can never be godly.

Paul helped us understand godliness by giving us a picture of ungodliness. In Romans 3:11–18, Paul examined the conditions of the unrighteous world by quoting a number of verses from the Old Testament:

> "There is none who understands;
> There is none who seeks after God.
> They have all turned aside;
> They have together become unprofitable;
> There is none who does good, no, not one."
> "Their throat is an open tomb;
> With their tongues they have practiced deceit;"
> "The poison of asps is under their lips;
> Whose mouth is full of cursing and bitterness."
> "Their feet are swift to shed blood;
> Destruction and misery are in their ways;
> And the way of peace have they not known."
> *"There is no fear of God before their eyes."* (emphasis mine)

The very essence of unrighteousness is the lack of a fear of God. As John MacArthur put it, "Man's true spiritual condition is nowhere more clearly seen than in the absence of a proper submission to and reverence for God."[2]

Everything that God wants you to be starts with your fearing Him. When the prophet Samuel anointed a youngster named David to be the future king of Israel, Scripture says "the Spirit of the Lord" was upon David. Isaiah prophesied that the same Spirit would be upon the coming Messiah. It is described in Isaiah 11:2 as the Spirit of wisdom, understanding, counsel, knowledge, might, and of the fear of the Lord. Isaiah even goes so far as to say Jesus' delight would be in the fear of the Lord (11:3). To fear God is to have His Spirit.

Every believer has some fear. For God to draw you to Himself through faith in His Son took some surrender and acknowledgement of His lordship on your part. But godliness is a constant process of divine revelation and response to that revelation. The more God reveals Himself to you, the more you should fear Him. And fear, like godliness, fleshes itself out in conduct.

God knew Abraham's fear of Him because Abraham did not withhold Isaac from Him. Job is described as a man who feared God, who was also blameless, upright, and one who "shunned evil." Telling God that He's wonderful and powerful is not fearing Him. To consider your conduct in light of how wonderful and powerful He is—now, that's fearing Him.

The lack of fear of God among people has been a source of great frustration, concern, and amazement for me. The core of much of the distorted portrait the world has of the contemporary Church is rooted in a fundamental lack of fear of God. Notice I speak specifically about the Church. I am not altogether surprised at the absence of fear in the world.

The Bible gives us much revelation concerning the characteristics of these last days. It speaks of the eyes of men being blinded, people having reprobate minds, and men walking in darkness. But the Word of God also speaks of tares and wheat, wolves in sheep's clothing, and sheep and goats, all in an attempt to paint an accurate image of the Church. However, I must confess that I have suffered periodically from an acute naïveté. For some reason, I expected things to be different in the Church.

Somewhere along the way many in the Church left the path toward God that begins with fear of Him. The distressing truth is that there persists within the ranks of soldiers of the cross a cancerous fearlessness that threatens the very heart of the family of faith. Within the ranks of the righteous, we have subtly bent exclusively toward the grace of God and disregarded the potential judgment of God. Many saints profess to love God without fearing Him. As a result, our way of life is frighteningly similar to that of the world, who, by definition, has little or no reverence for God.

I have wondered why the Lord has allowed me to see so much within the Body of Christ. I look back and often feel that I might have been stronger in my walk and further along in my spiritual development had I not been exposed to such blatant fearlessness in the lives of Christians, in general, and Christian leaders, in particular.

When I was fifteen, I was part of a gospel concert. I noticed how performers would go onstage and work the audience into a spiritual frenzy. Afterward, they would come backstage— already reeking of alcohol—cursing about the amount of money they would be paid, as they made their way to the hotel for the after-concert party.

I have attended denominational conventions and watched in disbelief as pastors and preachers—many of whom I either knew or knew of and respected—checked into hotel rooms with their girlfriends, while their wives were at home assuming their spouses were taking care of Kingdom business. I have known pastors who not only drank with their members, but who informed the interviewing pulpit committees that drinking was a part of their lifestyle. This pseudo-honesty was dwarfed by the content of the revelation itself. Not only was this information not a hindrance to their being called by the Church, but it became common knowledge among the congregation, who no doubt prided themselves with having such a liberal and nonjudgmental leader. The vain attempts to justify or cover unfaithfulness in high places are not only attacks on the testimony of the Church, but are also, at some level, expressions of fearlessness.

Holy fear is not an optional extra in your salvation package. It is more than a priority. It is essential. It is air to your spiritual lungs, blood to your veins. It is life, a fountain of life, according to Solomon (Prov. 14:27). To live without fear is to live without life. If that sounds extreme, remember that a lack of fear is ungodliness. And there is one end to ungodliness, and that is death (Ps. 1:6). But the godly are both protected and directed by their fear of God (Ps. 33:18–19).

The Planting of Fear

When a godly man or woman walks in the fear of the Lord, a divine pact is established. That pact is the fulfillment of a promise made by God to His people in Jeremiah 32:40. Through the prophet, God said, "I will make an everlasting covenant with them, that I will not turn away from doing them good; *but I will put My fear in their hearts so that they will not depart from Me*" (emphasis mine). A covenant is an agreement, a contract. Here, I believe God was saying, "I am going to be your God, and I will not leave you. I will be in your life for good. My thoughts of you are good. My actions toward you are good. In addition to that, I'm going to make a deposit into your spirit. I will place in your heart a fear of Me, a fear that will keep you from leaving Me."

God knows we are all sheep prone to wander from Him. All His sheep have gone astray and tried to seek their own way, but God said He will put something in you that is going to pull you back. In the final installment of *The Godfather* trilogy, an aging Michael Corleone reviewed his life of crime and declared, "Every time I tried to get out, something just pulled me back." God has planted His fear in us to the extent that when we feel like walking away, running away, or going our own way, we will be pulled back and challenged to live godly lives.

A godly life is one in which the believer loves the Lord so much, reveres Him so much, desires to please Him so much, that he actually is afraid to do something contrary to God. He is afraid to break the heart of God. He is afraid to sin. He is afraid to cheat. He is afraid to misuse others. He lives with this fear because God loved him enough to have planted this seed of fear within him.

God's covenant with us assures us that He's not going anywhere and ensures that we don't go anywhere either. His plan is to bless you so much while you're with Him that you will begin to see the contrast between living your life in His pleasure and living your life in disobedience. You will know the difference between living in fellowship with Him and living in rebellion against Him. You will know the difference between living at home and living in the far country. And when you venture into the land of disobedience and rebellion, the rebuke you receive for your defiance will not only drive you back to Him, but it will make you think a little longer and harder about straying in that manner again. He wants you to live your life so close to Him that you are afraid of the consequences of leaving Him.

I have a great respect for our Jewish brothers. One of the most rewarding experiences of my life was the blessed opportunity to study at Hebrew Union College and the University of Judaism. It was during my short time at these institutions that I gained such an appreciation of Jewish culture. I am particularly impressed and inspired by the Jews' deliberate actions to preserve the awareness of their special relationship with God.

One extraordinary aspect of Jewish culture is the wearing of phylacteries. In Deuteronomy 6:8, Moses told the Israelites to tie God's law on their hands and foreheads. Phylacteries are small cases containing certain passages of the law to be worn on the left hand and in the center of the forehead. They were then, and are still to orthodox Jews today, visible symbols of the perpetual awareness of the keeping of God's covenant in their hearts and minds.

Fear of God is at the very core of our relationship with Him. Why? It is impossible to have fellowship with God without godly fear. Why is it impossible to be godly without fear? Certainly, God is worthy of all the reverence and respect He demands, but I don't think that's why He demands it. God would still be God if none of us said He was or treated Him like He was.

I've heard preachers say God likes to have His holy ego stroked. That's why we worship Him. Please. When you are All, there is no place in you for the small of egotism. God does not need us, emotionally or otherwise. So, why does He want us to fear Him? I do not presume to know the mind of God, but there are two reasons Scripture points to, both of which are rooted in the Almighty's love for us.

First, fear is the only compass God gives us on this journey, which we cannot begin to understand. We know that we are going to live with Him, but we don't know how to get there. We know that we will be like Him, but we don't know how to fashion spirit from our corruptible flesh. He knows where we're going, but if we don't fear Him, we won't follow Him. He knows the plans He has for us and has the power to execute those plans. Without fear, we will go our own way and resist His hand on our lives because of the natural bent of rebellion that distinguishes man.

Second, fearing God means we don't have to fear anything or anyone else. You are being led by the One who sees everything, protected by the One who can do everything, provided for by the One who has everything, taught by the One who knows everything. Fearing God guarantees you refuge, comfort, peace, and joy in your trials. Nothing can overtake you.

The Lord told Joshua not to be afraid, because He was going before him. He let Mary know not to be afraid, because He was with her. He told the children of Israel not to be afraid and to remember all the trials He had brought them through. If God is before us, beside us, and behind us, what do we have to fear? Paul understood this when he said, "If God is for us, who can be against us?" (Rom. 8:31).

Corporate Fear

There are churches all over the world where the Holy Spirit is not present. He is not present because the people don't fear God. They may be socially active, economically viable, and organizationally functional; but where there is no fear, there is no godliness. Where there is no godliness, there is no anointing. There can be no comfort because God will never comfort you when you are outside His will.

People go to some churches week in and week out seeking to be comforted in their sin. You can find a church that makes you comfortable with its ritual, its tradition, and its ministry emphasis. But it is a tragedy if a church's leaders do not strain to create an atmosphere of godliness and the body does not fear God as it works out its salvation. The comfort one finds in that situation is one of the greatest deceptions of the devil.

Satan desires to make you comfortable in your sin. If you are comfortable in your sin, you will not see the need to confess it. If you do not confess your sin, you will not know the cleansing forgiveness of God. Without His cleansing forgiveness, you cannot enter into His presence, because your sin separates you from Him (Isa. 59:2). Then Satan has you right where he wants you—in sin and apart from God. If you are in sin and comfortable in your church, please know that you are being deceived by the enemy. God won't help you walk in sin. What He will do, however, is help you get up and walk away from that sin so that you might get back on the path of righteousness and walk in the fear of the Lord. He says if you walk in fear of Him, you will know the comfort of His Spirit and a fruitful, spiritually productive relationship with Him.

Philippians 2:12 says, "Therefore, my beloved, as you have always obeyed, not as in my presence only, but now much more in my absence, work out your own salvation with fear and trembling." Paul said work out your own salvation in a holy reverence for God and a righteous "afraid-ness" of Him. You don't work *for* your salvation; you work out your salvation. You don't work to get saved; you work because you are saved. Your salvation is fleshed out in a daily process of living in the power of the Spirit of God.

A remarkable thing happens when a church is full of godly men and women who work out their salvation with a fear of God. Acts 9:31 says, "Then the churches throughout all Judea, Galilee, and Samaria had peace and were edified." Now watch this: "And *walking in the fear of the Lord and in the comfort of the Holy Spirit,* they were multiplied" (emphasis mine). The church grew numerically and spiritually, quantitatively and qualitatively. Why? They did so because they walked in the fear of the Lord and in the comfort of the Holy Ghost. Walking in the comfort of the Holy Ghost does not mean shouting, running down aisles, laughing uncontrollably, barking like a dog, or jumping across benches. The comfort of the Holy Ghost is that ministry of the Spirit that stabilizes you. It is the settling of your spirit by His Spirit. It is when God strengthens you by coming alongside you in your particular set of circumstances.

The context of the Acts 9 text suggests that at the time this comfort settled on the aforementioned believers, the church was suffering intense persecution. Christians were sought and killed for following a man named Jesus. But in spite of their oppression, they were edified and growing individually and collectively. They were growing because the Holy Spirit was comforting them, and there would have been no comfort without fear.

By the way, fellow pastor, how is your church growing? If it is alive, it ought to be growing. If it is not growing, maybe God is calling you to examine the spiritual atmosphere in your congregation. Dear pastor, maybe God is telling you to examine your own lifestyle and your own heart. Now, don't take my position to the extreme. I am by no means suggesting that the only gauge for vitality and growth in a church is the size of its roll. Last year, I spoke at a Promise Keepers gathering in the Oakland Coliseum to more than sixty thousand men. I remember being impressed at how the workers and staff of the Coliseum operated so efficiently and excellently. The way they managed the facilities, the crowd, the parking, and the lights and sound was remarkable—wow! I was impressed until I overheard one of the workers talking to one of the attendees. The worker said, "We do this every weekend." Then it dawned on me. In spite of the fantastic achievement of getting sixty thousand men together in one place in Jesus' name, that venue sees that many people every weekend the Raiders are in town. We did it for one weekend. They do it every week.

The world will always "out crowd" the church. Crowds have assembled for every reason, from viewing the tail of a comet to supporting a follower of Mohammed. Don't measure the godliness of a church by the size of the crowd. The Bible says "narrow is the gate and difficult is the way which leads to life, and there are few who find it" (Matt. 7:14). Don't count bodies. Count lives. See if the people followed Jesus into the assembly or if they followed some other leader. See if there is a holy, reverential fear of God woven into the fabric of their behavior. A growing church is filled with people who walk in the fear of the Lord. Because they fear the Lord, they know the comfort of the Holy Ghost. This is the path to godliness and growth in any church. How is your church growing?

A Portrait of Fear

Awhile back, my son, Kendan, got into trouble in school. He knew his teacher had already called home with a very bad report on him. So when he got home, he came straight to my study. He peeped in at me from across the room, afraid to come close. He knew he had broken Daddy's law. He had already been punished at school, and he knew he was about to get punished by me. He moved ever so cautiously toward me with tears already wetting his cheeks. I explained that his behavior was totally unacceptable. He had called another kid a bad name. He had disrespected his classmate, his teacher, and me. He hadn't realized that whenever he goes outside, he's representing his family. After the mandatory tongue lashing, I punished him. He got what he feared.

Three hours or so later when his period of punishment had been completed, just before he was about to go to bed, he came back to the same door and looked at me long enough to make eye contact. I stretched out my arms. He ran to me and jumped up into my lap, gave me the biggest bear hug his tiny arms could manage, and said, "I love you, Daddy." I said, "I love you, Kendan. I love you so very much."

You see, I try to teach him that the basis of my discipline is my love for him. That is also the way of the Lord.

The God we fear in times of trouble is the same God we can

run to for consolation. When you get into trouble, don't be like Adam and Eve. Don't run away from God. Run to Him instead. You can run to Him because He loves you. He loves you enough to chastise you. The enemy tries to mess with your mind by telling you God won't forgive your bad deeds. But even though you messed up, you can come and take your seat on His divine lap—as His child. That is where He wants you, because He loves you, because He's your Daddy.

Prayer for Godly Fear

Gift me with the knowledge to understand Your
ways and the wisdom to walk in that
knowledge.
Make me an encouragement to those who
seek You.
Lord, make us, Your church, always aware of
Your greatness and always grateful for
Your unending mercy.
Give us a craving for the comfort of the Holy
Spirit.
Help us grow, Lord.
In Jesus' name, Amen.

Chapter 3 Exercises

Exercise 1: Salvation

Memorize Philippians 2:12: "Work out your own salvation with fear and trembling."

As you repeat this verse to yourself, think about your salvation. How important is it to you? Have you ever considered what your life would be like if it were not available to you? Imagine that it is a precious, fragile thing held in the palm of your hand, entrusted to your care. How do you nurture your salvation? How do you water it? Its flower is Life Eternal. Does knowing this change your idea of the importance of working out God's gift of salvation?

Solomon was the wisest man who ever lived. Solomon feared God. In fact, he tells us in Proverbs 9:10 that wisdom begins with fearing God. But Solomon isn't the only God-fearing saint mentioned in Scripture. Look up the following references:

- Abraham: Genesis 22:12
- The first judges: Exodus 18:21
- Job: Job 1:1
- Cornelius: Acts 10:22
- You and me: Hebrews 12:28

Exercise 2: The Boss of You

Have you ever seen a defiant child? Nose raised, chin jutted out, hand on hip, the child declares, "You're not the boss of me!" It seems almost impossible to imagine someone doing that to God, but we do. Every time we knowingly disobey Him, we're telling Him we're less concerned with what He wants and more concerned with what we want. In other words, we don't fear Him enough to let Him be the boss. Complete the following statements:

I was dishonest when I _____

I was selfish when I _____

I was prideful when I_____

I was gossiping when I_____

I was impatient when I _____

I was inconsiderate when I _____

I was unkind when I _____

Now reread each statement, replacing the first part with "I did not fear God when I . . ." Focus on the lack of fear, which resulted in sin, rather than the sin itself. It's hard to believe we would have the nerve to defy God, but we do so every day of our lives. Try to see sin as an act of standing before God and telling Him He's not your boss. Now direct these statements to God. Tell Him, "Lord, I did not fear you when I . . ." If you haven't already, confess each sin and repent of it. Appropriate God's forgiveness for it.

Remember that disobedience is a by-product of a lack of fear. A lack of fear is a by-product of a lack of knowledge. Don't beat yourself up about it. Decide to get to know Him better.

Exercise 3: If God Be for You

Fearing God means never having to fear anything else. The correct attitude toward God always places you on a path toward Him, allowing you access to His protection. The Bible says that as children of God, we are to be anxious for nothing and let God handle everything. Following is a list of common fears. Look up the Scripture for any fear you struggle with.

Rejection	Hebrews 13:5–6
Poverty	Philippians 4:19
Death	1 Thessalonians 4:13–18
The unknown	Jeremiah 29:11
Making mistakes	Romans 8:28

Now take these issues, and any others you might have, and combine them with the appropriate Scriptures to make a positive confession. For example:

I am not afraid of making mistakes because God says all things work together for the good of those who love Him and are called according to His purpose. I am not afraid of the unknown, because God knows the thoughts He has for me. They are thoughts of peace and not of evil, and they give me hope.

Write your positive confessions below, including those not listed above. Memorize them if you can. The sword of the Spirit is the Word of God. Use it.

_____

_____

_____

_____

_____

Exercise 4: The Fruits of Fear

Solomon knew that the fear of the Lord is so much more than the beginning of wisdom. Look at the following Scriptures from the wise king's proverbs and list the fruit produced from a healthy, holy fear of God.

Proverbs 10:27_____

Proverbs 14:26_____

Proverbs 14:27_____

Proverbs 15:16_____

Proverbs 19:23_____

Proverbs 28:14_____

Chapter 4
The Challenge of Godliness

His divine power has given to us all things that pertain to life and godliness.

2 Peter 1:3

Some of you have read this far, and you have decided that godliness is not God's plan for you. You've determined that godliness is a distinction bestowed on an anointed few—the super saints, the godly Green Berets. You may have spotted one or two of these consecrated commandos at your church, and you're convinced that their relationship with God is on an entirely different level. They're navigating the deep waters of divine revelation, keeping company with the mysteries of the Kingdom. You, on the other hand, are still wearing water wings, splashing around in the spiritual baby pool singing "Jesus Loves Me." They have hidden God's Word in their hearts. God's Word is hidden to you, too, but only because you haven't learned how to use the index in your Bible yet. They struggle with the weight of their anointing. You struggle to get through a day of work without cussing out somebody. God sees your struggle, my brother. He feels your pain, my sister. And He still expects your walk to be godly.

It seems unfair, especially when you consider the disparity that exists with human beings. There are distinctions between us and among us. We are compartmentalized, departmentalized, labeled, and overtly or covertly ranked, then expected to perform accordingly.

A few years ago, a major car company advertised its luxury model with the slogan, "We were all born equal, but we don't stay that way." How telling. God seems to encourage the unevenness by bestowing different gifts upon His children in differing degrees, at different times, and for different purposes. How, then, can He require us all to run the same race, at the same level, and for the same prize when we are not the same?

We are the same in two significant ways: (1) Apart from Him, all of us can do nothing; and (2) with Him, we can do all things. God is the great equalizer, and we praise Him for not expecting us to be godly by ourselves. Godliness is not only expected of us by God, it is attainable by us with God. It doesn't matter who you are or who you aren't. Man, woman, tall, short, big Bible, little Bible—it doesn't matter, because as the Scriptures say in 2 Peter 1:3, we have everything we need for life and godliness!

That just blows me away. Every time I read that verse, something grips my spirit. I already have everything I need to live and to live godly. I have all I need to be a godly pastor, husband, and father.

Everything you need to be a godly husband, wife, friend, professional, boyfriend, girlfriend, daughter, or teacher—God has already given to you. God has equipped you with tools to overcome every challenge you'll ever face. You're ready to climb every mountain in your path. That blesses me, because I know how unequipped I was for this journey. On my own I was blind, deaf, and lame. On my own I could only produce unrighteousness. On my own I would choose death. But God has given me life, and He didn't stop there. He gave me godliness. My godly goal is no longer up in the clouds somewhere. It's not some ethereal, intangible, unreachable, theoretical concept. Godliness is available to us; it's ours for the taking. It is real, flesh and bones. It walks and talks. Godliness is in our faces daring us to give it a try and realize the fullness of it.

How will we meet the challenge of godliness? How do we appropriate everything that God has given to us for godliness? And what exactly does everything include?

The first thing we were given was a model in Jesus Christ. Through knowing Him we gain the means and the method for acquiring godliness.

The Model: Jesus Christ

God's goal for us is godliness. The means He uses to measure our godliness—the acceptable minimum level of performance—is Jesus. I'm not always comfortable with that. There are days when I'd rather not have to shoot for that Jesus-level. There are days, for example, when I'd like to shoot for the David-level. David was a man after God's heart, but sometimes he was selfish. I have been selfish. Moses was a friend of God's, even though he got angry. I have been angry. Abraham's faith was counted unto him as righteousness, but the Bible says he lied. I have lied. Peter, the rock, was proud. Paul had a sinful past. Even Job questioned God. Jacob wrestled with Him.

These are lives that, at one time or another, look more like mine. These are marks I seem more likely to hit. But David-ness or Moses-ness or even Abraham-ness is not God's desire for me. Godliness is. And the only perfect model for that is His perfect Son, Jesus.

Second Peter 1:3 says that we have everything we need for godliness through a knowledge of Jesus Christ. Knowledge, as expressed by Peter, is a two-fold concept. It comprises informational and relational understanding. We cannot truly know Jesus unless we know him from both of these perspectives. To neglect one of them is to invite the Savior to share in a communion of superficiality.

Knowing Christ Informationally

Don't ever discount the facts about Christ. The data alone on Him is staggering. He's the Son of God. He was there, in the beginning, with God. He is God. He became flesh. His life fulfilled over three hundred prophecies. He was born of a virgin. He turned water to wine. He healed the lame, blind, and demon-possessed. He fed thousands. He saved the world. And that's just an overview.

John said if we were to write a resumé for Jesus and include everything He was and did, the world could not contain the content of it (John 21:25).

Knowing Christ from an informational perspective is crucial. Your walk with God should never take place solely at gut level. Be wary of saints who always feel the presence of God and don't spend time studying the Word of God. Walking with God is not a feeling. Worship is not emotion. Godliness is not a sensation. We are transformed by the renewing of our minds. What you feel should be a function of what you know about Jesus, not the other way around.

Our knowledge of Christ is our pattern. What we know about who He is and how He acts tells us how we are to be and act. Jesus loved His enemies. We're supposed to love ours. He prayed, fasted, studied, and meditated. So should we. He was singularly devoted to doing the will of God. He was meek, merciful, and longsuffering. We should be all those things. He was a man made of flesh and blood. He made it possible for us to be all those things. And when it seems impossible, we need to know that Jesus was tempted, afraid, angry, discouraged, and suffered just like we do. But know, too, that He called upon the Lord to give Him grace to endure all that He suffered. And we know that God was always faithful.

I wonder how much of our suffering could be averted if we just knew a little more about Jesus. If we knew no one could pluck us out of Christ's hand, could we be afraid when somebody told us we were going to hell for struggling in sin? Sister, if you knew that He chose, taught, and loved Judas, could you be devastated when somebody you loved stabbed you in the back? Brother, if you knew that He saved somebody dying on the cross next to Him, would you be too ashamed to ask "What must I do to be saved?"

Knowing Christ Relationally

Your informational knowledge of Jesus is your roadmap to godliness. But a roadmap has no value if you don't want to take the journey. Informational knowledge tells you who Jesus is, and the outgrowth of that is direction toward godliness. Relational knowledge tells you who Jesus is to you and the outgrowth of that is a desire for godliness.

To know Jesus is to love him. The more you know how much He sacrificed for you, the more you'll love Him. When you look through your sanctified imagination and see Him hanging there on that cross, you are reminded that He hung up there for you. He was not there for His sins, but for yours. Now, if you don't love Jesus, it's because you don't know Him. But, if you do know Him, you can't help but love Him. And the more you love Him, the more committed you will be to Him. The more committed you are to Him, the more you'll want to live your life for Him. The more you want to live your life for Him, the more like Him you will become.

God first showed us what godliness looks like through Christ's example. Then He gave us what we need to attain it. He gives us two things. The first is His power. The Bible says in 2 Peter 1:3, "His divine power has given to us all things that pertain to life and godliness." The second thing He has given you is His promise. Verse 4 says, "By which have been given to us exceedingly great and precious promises, that through these you may be partakers of the divine nature." God said that by His power and based on His promise, you can be a partaker in His very nature. Think about that powerful statement. The word *partaker* means "to share in something." Another translation says, "that we may participate in the divine nature." Godliness is not just God-centeredness, godliness is God-likeness. It is sharing in the likeness of the very character of God, which is accomplished through the gift of His power and promises.

His Power

How does God's power work in our lives? The most vivid picture of this process is found in Colossians 1:29: "To this end I also labor, striving according to His working which works in me mightily." Here, Paul talked about living a life in accordance with the will of God.

Together the words *labor, striving, working,* and *mightily* give us a complete picture of God's power and how it operates in us. Paul said he was laboring. The essence of the word *labor* means "to be weary, fatigued, or tired." It means "to toil." Now the word *striving* means "to struggle or strain." It is the picture of an athlete or competitor struggling to make every effort to achieve his goal. It implies overcoming obstacles and pain in straining toward the goal. In other words, Paul implied that godliness is not a cakewalk. It is not something that just happens to you as you bask in the glory of being God's child. It takes effort on your part. Paul labored. He strove. He competed, and he got tired. But in spite of his fatigue, he kept on struggling. He kept on striving.

How did he do that? He strove according to the working of God in him. The word *working* is the English translation of *energeia*, the Greek word from which we get our word *energy*. It means "effective operation or activity." Paul said that he was striving and straining and struggling according to God's *energeia*. He was tired and fatigued, but God operated within him, energizing him and pushing him toward the mark.

That push was not some little nudge. This verse about Paul laboring according to God's working ends with the phrase "which works in me mightily." That last word, *mightily*, is the translation of the Greek word *dunamis*, from which we get our word *dynamite*. It means "ability." Here's what I believe Paul implied: "God not only gives me the energy to do what I'm too tired to do or what I'm struggling to do, He also gives me the ability to do it."

I preach four sermons each Sunday. Our sanctuary is not large enough to hold the entire congregation at one time, so we have four services a day. People, fellow preachers especially, ask me how I do it each week. My answer is always the same. I don't. When I started pastoring, I had about six people to preach to. God gave me what I needed to feed them.

Twenty years later, I'm still in the preaching business because God is still in the feeding business. I labor now as I did then. I strive, struggle, and strain now as I did then. Sometimes I get weary. But I continue doing what I do and love doing it, by the way, despite my weariness. God always gives me a dose of His energy, then infuses me with His dynamite ability. Six folks have become six thousand. As long as I let God's *energeia* and *dunamis* do their thing, no one will go hungry.

Part of godliness is understanding that we can do nothing with our own strength. Once you realize the power you have access to as God's child, you won't want to do anything by yourself.

Godliness doesn't mean you will not struggle. In fact, it's a guarantee that you will (1 Peter 4:12). But when you do, ask yourself, "Is what I'm going through bigger than Jesus hanging on a cross?" Is there anything anybody will go through that's bigger than that? Because the power God uses to energize us is the same power He used to raise Jesus from the tomb and give Him dominion over everything (Eph. 1:19–22). If you don't have a struggle that's bigger than our Savior on the cross, God's power can get you through it.

His Promise

The phrase "God's promises" sounds almost redundant, if you think about it. What is a promise but words sent forth with a guarantee of performance attached? There is nothing that God says that He will not also perform (Isa. 55:11). There is nothing God says that does not tell the truth about who He is (Heb. 6:18). God does not only make promises; He is Himself a promise.

The promises referred to in 2 Peter 1:4 are summed up by Paul in his letter to the church at Philippi: "He who has begun a good work in you will complete it until the day of Jesus Christ" (Phil. 1:6).

The day of Jesus Christ points to the day when Christ comes for you or you go to meet Him. Everything in between now and then is part of the process of completing the good work in you. That work began when you accepted Christ into your life. Notice I didn't say the work began because you accepted Christ.

Salvation is not your making a commitment to God; salvation is your accepting God's promise to conform you to the image of His Son. Like the power of God, the promise finds its source and substance in God alone. He began the work, and He's going to complete it. The great thing about God's promises is that they are always, always, always kept. You can take them to the bank because the promises of God are inseparable from the power of God. He's not going to stop moving in you, around you, or on your behalf until you look just like Jesus. He's not going to leave you half-done, half-baked, half-cooked, or half-completed. And you have His word on it.

That's why you must be careful about judging people when you see them. You see me as I am now, but God sees me for what I'm becoming. You don't see what I used to be. You don't know that God is still working on me. If you think I'm in bad shape today, you should have seen me before God got His hands on me. God snatched me out of my ungodliness, stood me on a rock of righteousness, then filled me with the power of His Spirit. His power is working in me giving me the ability to do what I could never have done without Him. And He will continue this process of sanctification in my life until Christ comes back.

We are now the sons and daughters of God. It does not appear what we shall be, but we do know that when He shall appear, we shall be like Him.

The Method: Adding and Subtracting

God not only gives us a model of godliness in Jesus Christ, but also the means to attain it in His power and promises. He also gives us a method by which to operate—adding and subtracting. Second Peter 1:5–7 says:

But also for this very reason, giving all diligence, add to your faith virtue, to virtue knowledge, to knowledge self-control, to self-control perseverance, to perseverance godliness, to godliness brotherly kindness, and to brotherly kindness love.

This is not just a process of addition; it is a progression as well. The order of adding is as important as the adding itself. We start with faith. Grace saves you through your faith, but you will never be a godly person if you stop at the level of saving faith. Salvation does not automatically make you a godly person. To your faith, you add virtue, which is courage and fortitude. It is that God-given quality that embodies our resolve to follow Christ. Once we have virtue, we add knowledge or our active pursuit of God through an understanding of His Word and its application in our lives. It is that knowledge that leads to temperance or self-control. Once we have temperance, we can be patient, which is the ability to endure through circumstances because we are no longer driven by the unchecked passions and desires that rule our carnal nature. And patience, said James, when it has had its perfect work, makes us complete, which is godliness. Only when we walk in godliness are we able to effectively show brotherly kindness and ultimately pure, godly charity or love.

Now don't make the mistake of focusing on the addition in verses 5 through 7 without first stopping by the required subtraction in verse 4. Verse 4 says, "having escaped the corruption that is in the world." In other words, don't try to add godliness without subtracting worldliness. Adding godliness without subtracting worldliness equals hypocrisy. A person who does this might see a brother fall and kick him all the way down. When you add without subtracting, you become the type of person who looks down your nose at people who do the same things you used to do before you found Jesus. When you're able to pray with people and still spread gossip about them, you haven't subtracted enough.

The goal is to keep adding and subtracting until we start to take on the character of God. Character always controls conduct. Conduct never controls character. If your godliness is a function of your conduct and not your character, then what you have is not godliness. What you have is a reputation. A reputation is governed by what people say you are. Your character is who you really are. Godliness is conduct that flows from character. I am who I am, so I do what I do.

Putting It All Together

How do you do what God has called you to do, even when you don't know how to do it? Or let's say you do know how, and you simply don't want to. The power of almighty God is the only answer.

Let's go over the steps again. It starts with knowing the model: Jesus. We can't settle for a life that falls short of Him, no matter how close we come or how far everybody else is behind us. The more I know Him, the more I know how much He loves me. I cannot know His love without experiencing His forgiveness. He forgave me before I ever asked Him. Imagine that.

If I told you that tomorrow someone would break into your house and violate you and all you stood for, could you forgive him today? When he got to your house and hurt you as planned, would you have love for him? This is the model of Jesus Christ.

With that model comes a desire to please Him, which becomes progressively more possible as I subtract my worldly attitudes and add spiritual ones. Then, once I determine, yes, I will forgive that person as an act of my will, God says, "You don't have enough forgiveness in you to forgive him or her. So, here, take some of Mine." And He energizes me with His power and forgiveness, and I can show that to the other person. That is godliness. God has set the standard and then commits Himself to giving us the power to meet it. Godliness is not perfection. It is continually striving with His power.

I want so much to be a godly father. I don't always know what that looks like. So, I trust the promises of God, knowing He will give me a father's heart. I trust that if my children say nothing else about me, they would say, "He was a godly father."

I want to be a godly husband. I don't always know what that looks like. So, I trust the promise of God to teach me how to cherish my wife and give my life to her the way Christ gave His for the Church.

I want most of all to be a godly pastor. I don't always know what that looks like. So, I trust the promises of God to never leave me, nor forsake me. I have everything I need to be a godly father, husband, and pastor. You have everything you need to be all that God wants you to be. You are fully equipped to live a life of godliness.

Prayer
for
Divine Revelation

Father, You are my sufficiency.
You have given me everything I need to be and
to do all that would please You.
I purpose in my heart to know You intimately.
Please show me the truth about You and give
me the power to walk in that truth.
Lord, continue to give me the ability and energy
to add to my faith until You are satisfied
with me.
Open my eyes that I might see my completeness
in You by faith, even as I walk in
imperfection.
Lord, make my struggle an example to others.
Make my striving a testament to Your
faithfulness.
Move in me and through me so my brothers and
sisters can see Your power.
Be glorified by all that you make of me.
In Jesus' name, Amen.

Chapter 4 Exercises

Exercise 1: What Is Godliness?

Memorize 2 Peter 1:3: "[He] has given to us all things that pertain to life and godliness, through the knowledge of Him who called us by glory and virtue."

We have everything we need to be godly through our knowledge of God and Christ. That knowledge is both informational and relational. Informational Knowledge: What you know about God and Jesus. Relational Knowledge: What you do with what you know about God and Jesus.

Our knowledge of God gives us access to His promises and power. These are the means by which we attain godliness. "God's promises" is almost redundant, when you think about it. God Himself is a promise. "God's power" also is redundant. You cannot separate God from either one of these ideas about Him. His promises are kept the moment He speaks them (Isa. 55:11), and His power is the vehicle that guarantees His promise (Eph. 1:18–19). Knowing this, we recognize that everything God says to us and about us will come to pass. If you do not see the promises of God manifested in your life, it's not because He hasn't kept them; it's because He hasn't revealed them to you yet.

Godliness goes beyond the faith that saved you. It is the power of God to change you by adding to faith virtue, knowledge, self-control, patience, and love, among other things. God loved you enough to save you, and He loves you too much to let you stay the same.

Pray about these things.

Exercise 2: Everything I Need

Peter says we have everything we need to be godly. Paul says we are complete in Christ. Jesus says if you accept Him, you receive eternal life. Still, most of us can look at our lives and see areas we'd like to improve. Look at the fruit of the Spirit in Galatians 5:22–23, the Beatitudes in Matthew 5:3–11, and Proverbs 3:1–10. Then list the things you would like to see the Lord improve in you.

_____   _____

_____   _____

_____   _____

_____   _____

_____   _____

Now, read Philippians 1:6. Insert each item on the list into it. For example, if patience is on your list, you would read the verse as, "He who has begun the work of patience in me will complete it."

Exercise 3: Like Father, Like Son, Like Me

List Jesus' traits. Be specific and use descriptive terms. For example: kind, nurturing, obedient, righteous, strong, Spirit-filled, powerful, etc.

_____   _____

_____   _____

_____   _____

_____   _____

_____   _____

It's one thing to know that God will make changes in you. It's another thing entirely to understand that He will conform you to the image of His perfect Son! Jesus is not only all the things you described above; He is all of them to perfection. This is God's plan for you. Read Romans 8:29. Then look at your list again, inserting each trait into the verse and applying it to you. Again using the example of patience, "I am predestined to be as patient as Jesus Christ." Don't rush through this exercise. We all really need to understand that God's plan is to make us look like Jesus. Nothing less will satisfy Him. Take a moment to pray and thank God for His Son, and thank Jesus for His example.

Chapter 5
The Assignment of Godliness

"Teacher, which is the great commandment in the law?" Jesus said to him, "'You shall love the LORD your God with all your heart, with all your soul, and with all your mind.' This is the first and great commandment. And the second is like it: 'You shall love your neighbor as yourself.' On these two commandments hang all the Law and the Prophets."

Matthew 22:36–40

When I was in college, I was assigned a paper by one of my toughest professors. Everyone had problems in this man's class, but I was determined to impress him. I decided he was going to remember me as the student who met his challenge and exceeded all his expectations. I worked on that paper like no other. It was well researched, well written, and turned in well before the deadline. I was excited about it, and I knew my professor would be too.

When I got it back, I was shocked to find a big red "F" on the title page. How did this happen? I looked through the paper for comments. I saw only positive ones. Then I came to the last page. "Great paper!" he wrote, "but this was not the assignment."

I was crushed. It was the most painful grade I had ever gotten. Not only had I failed, but I had succeeded wonderfully in my failing. All *i*'s had been dotted. All *t*'s had been crossed. My ability to do the work was not in question. But I was so bent on proving myself worthy to do the assignment that I became the focus, not the assignment. Had I been more concerned with pleasing my professor than impressing him, I may have fared better.

Some of you are trying to live godly lives. Your efforts to that end, though well-intended and on some levels effective, are misdirected. You give your money and time to every visible cause, quote Scripture eloquently, pray piously, and never miss a Communion. One day, Jesus is going to return to earth to claim His lambs, and there you'll stand, poised to receive your crown of glory. He may say, "I'm sorry, but all that giving and quoting and praying—that wasn't the assignment I gave you." One day we will all have to give an account to God for how we lived our lives. Our work will only stand up if it answers affirmatively to two questions: (1) Did we love the Lord with all our heart, soul, and mind? and (2) Did we love our neighbor as ourselves? Nothing else will matter. That is the assignment. There is no grade, only pass or fail.

In Matthew 22:36, Jesus was asked about the great, or most important, commandment in the law. He replied, "'You shall love the LORD your God with all your heart, with all your soul, and with all your mind.' This is the first and great commandment. And the second is like it: 'You shall love your neighbor as yourself.' On these two commandments hang all the Law and the Prophets." Understand this. The entire Hebrew Bible was comprised of the Law and the Prophets. The Law was the first five books, which is also called the Torah. The rest of it was the writings of the prophets. So when Christ said "on these two commandments hang all the Law and the Prophets," He was saying there is nothing required in all of Scripture that cannot be understood or fulfilled in the doing of these two commandments.

So when we consider the requirements of godliness, we recognize that conduct consistent with the character of God must also fall completely within the perimeters set down by Jesus in this passage.

Loving God

As Jesus commanded, loving God is the most important thing we can do. But Jesus qualified the extent of love He was looking for.

With All Your Heart, Soul, and Mind: Commitment

What does it mean to love God with all your heart, soul, and mind? In a word, it means commitment. It means starting with God and ending with Him. It means considering Him before everything else—your mate, your children, your job, your boss, your mortgage, and yourself. Your heart, soul, and mind comprise the whole of you, and God wants all of you. Don't ever make the mistake of thinking He'll accept most of you. Don't ever measure the strength of your commitment to Him by the yardstick of other saints. If they're giving 20 percent and you're giving 80, they may be impressed with you, but God isn't.

The literal meaning of *commit* is to "send with" or "connect." It is the idea of attaching one thing to another with the intention that the one attached will go with the one it is attached or committed to. For example, you can't put five dollars in your child's hand and send his hand to the store. You send him with the money.

Likewise, when you committed your life to Christ, you committed everything to Him, whether you act like it or not. Some of us want to commit Sundays to God and act like Mondays through Saturdays belong to us. Others are happy to commit our finances to Him, but keep Him away from an ungodly relationship in our lives. Some wives want to commit their husband's lack of direction and provision to God, but stop short at committing their own lack of submission. Some husbands are willing to commit their wife's uncontrolled tongue, but not their obligation to cherish her. Commitment is an all or nothing proposition. Either you are or you aren't. Being half committed, partly committed, and sort of committed, is like being half-dead, partly pregnant, and sort of saved.

Commitment also implies agreement. "Can two walk together, unless they are agreed?" (Amos 3:3). When you commit your life to God, you're saying you agree with Him in all things. You agree that He is all that He says He is. You agree to walk with Him, go where He goes, stay on His path, keep up to His pace, and be what He requires you to be. Godliness is agreeing with God. It is committing your life, your conduct, and your condition to Him consistently.

Now notice the focus of your commitment. You are committed to God—not to the things He has called you to do, not to the people He has put in your life. Where most of us err is by committing ourselves to everything but God. We seek things to do for Him, but we forget that He told us to seek Him first.

Jesus explained that one day He's going to throw a big party in heaven for His brothers and sisters, and some folks are going to try to crash it. They're going to say, "Our invitation must've gotten lost in the mail. We should be on the list. We prophesied and cast out demons in Your name."

But Jesus is going to tell them they can't party with Him. Even though they knew how to act saved, they didn't know the Savior. Always remember that your commitment is to Christ, and all other things flow from there.

Christians burn out because their commitment is misdirected. You'll hear people say they "overcommit" themselves. I would suggest that if you have more than one commitment in your life, you are overcommitted.

This is how it works. We commit ourselves to God and God alone. Then He commits Himself to us. He commits all that He is to us. He makes Himself and His power and His wisdom available to us. His peace is available, as are His joy, His hope, His holiness, and His godliness. We can do all that He calls us to do by His commitment to us.

What have we committed to Him? Our hearts, minds, and souls.

We must commit our hearts. We commit our heart to God when we align our thoughts, reasoning, judgment, and emotions with His. When our desires are in agreement with the desires of God, our heart is committed to Him. When we are tempted to hurt someone who hurts us, our committed heart prays. When we are tempted to compromise at work, our committed heart walks through the fire of ridicule and persecution according to the Word of God. A committed heart weeps with those who weep and rejoices with those who rejoice. A committed heart chooses compassion over condemnation. A committed heart listens for God and listens to Him.

To commit your heart means also to submit it to the scrutiny of the Holy Spirit, allowing Him to expose and eliminate all darkness. Jeremiah said the heart is wicked and deceitful. In fact, John said the only reason we can love God is because He first loved us. God is love. So when we walk with God, we love Him. Our hearts are in agreement with His. We go where He goes. We feel what His heart feels.

We must commit our minds. Our mind is committed to God when we refuse to operate in any understanding that does not agree with the mind of God. A mind that loves God completely thinks the way God thinks. It processes information the way God processes it. Solomon knew the thoughts of a committed mind are established by God (Prov. 16:3). In other words, when we love the Lord with all our mind, He shows us how to see the world as He sees it. He shows us Jesus. When we commit our mind to God, He lets us get inside His head. We don't have to wonder how Jesus would handle a situation. We know.

We must commit our souls. Understanding how to love God with our soul is difficult to grasp because *soul* in English has a somewhat vague meaning to most people.

The word *soul* in Matthew 22 and the word *life* in Matthew 10 and John 10 are from the same Greek word, *psuche*. The key to understand loving God with the soul is found in Matthew 10 and John 10, where *psuche* is translated "life."

Remember, Jesus said in Matthew 22:37 that we are to love the Lord with all our soul. In Matthew 10:39, He said, "He who finds his life will lose it, and he who loses his life for My sake will find it." In John 10:11, He said, "I am the good shepherd. The good shepherd gives His life for the sheep."

The meaning of *life* here is not simply the period from birth until death, but the essence of what gives our bodies life or animation. It is the difference between a corpse and a live body. At a funeral, when you look at a corpse of someone you knew, you recognize instantly that his soul, that which made him alive, is gone.

How then do you love the Lord with your life? You do what Jesus did. You give it up. You give up your life for Christ's sake the same way He gave up His for your sake. You lay it down. You lose it. You relinquish control of it to the will of God, just like the Lamb of God. A soul that loves God completely claims no rights to life for itself. A soul committed to God agrees to die, so that God might live through him. Are you willing to give up your life for God?

The BOW Principle

Do you love the Lord with all your heart, mind, and soul? If you're still wondering, a simple test will help you determine this. Ask yourself this question: To whom do you bow? Whom do you (B)elieve, (O)bey, and (W)orship? If you love the Lord completely, you should be BOW-ing to Him and Him alone.

Believe Him. God gives us all a measure of faith. Where we put it is up to us. Believing God is not in your mind. It is in your behavior. Even the faith that saved you manifested itself in the act of your asking Christ to be your Savior. Too often we mistake trust for belief. Belief is "trust in action." If we believe God—truly believe Him—it will be evident in our lives. Godliness, in part, is a desire to please God. The writer of Hebrews said that without faith, or belief in action, it is impossible to please Him.

Obey Him. The Bible says that if we love the Lord, we'll keep His commandments. If there are areas in your life where you persist in disobedience, God says you don't love Him. He didn't say your love for Him is doubtful or that maybe you don't love Him as much as you should. He says you don't—no ifs, ands, or buts. Now that's a hard word for those who want to be godly and have issues with compromise. But remember, our hearts are wicked and incapable of real love without God showing us how to love. So, the only way we can love Him properly is to follow His lead, which is to obey Him.

Worship Him. Worship is not what you do from nine to eleven o'clock every Sunday. It's what you are twenty-four hours, seven days a week. Worshiping God is living a life bright with the flame of sacrifice and obedience to Him. It is allowing everything in your life—your family, your marriage, your job—to be what you lay on the altar. Doing all things to the glory of God is your altar. Allowing the glory of God to consume you for all the world to see—that is worship. When God asks us to worship

Him, He's not asking us to come to church and say nice things about Him. That's praise. Worship involves offering up something to God.

Paul said that something is to be you.

Loving One Another

Jesus' command to love the Lord is summed up in commitment. His command to love others is summed up in ministry. Jesus says we are to love our neighbor as ourselves. If I love myself, I desire my needs to be met. Now, if I love you the way God wants me to, my desire will be to meet your needs.

Meeting the needs of others is ministry. Ministry is being involved in the edification of the lives of others. It is serving others. Jesus said He came to minister, not to be ministered to. If we're going to love one another like Jesus, we've got to enter one another's lives the way He did.

Ministry means "being a channel of God's love." It means that because God has loved me, I will now love others. As He has given to me, I will give to others. The most selfish thing you can do is take the love of God and keep it for yourself. You are to be a channel for His love. You are to be a minister. That means more than just collecting information, filling up notebooks, or writing bits of wisdom in the margin of your Bible. God wants you involved in the lives of other people. He wants you to receive His love, then pass it on.

My job as a pastor, according to Ephesians 4:12, is the "equipping of the saints for the work of ministry." I am not the minister. You are. I'm the pastor. You're the minister. I equip you to be what God has called you to be. If your pastor has done his job right, rather if God has done His job through your pastor, you will be eager to touch lives the way Jesus touched them.

True ministry requires a servant's heart. Servitude is not a job description. It's a mind-set that needs to be cultivated in order to minister effectively to the body of Christ. When Peter and the other disciples were arguing about who was greatest in the kingdom, the King of kings doffed his clothes and donned a towel to wash their feet, the lowliest of tasks.

Now, Jesus knew who He was—the Son of God, the one with the highest position of all. But true to His nature, He put that position aside. True ministry means shedding your position so that you might serve. It means giving up title and entitlement to see to the needs of another. Your station ceases to be an issue, and so does theirs. There is no one too high to serve and no one too low to be served because Jesus Christ, the Name above all names, the One to whom every knee would bow and every tongue would confess lordship, became of no reputation to serve us. The highest became the lowest that we might have an example to follow. And as long as we fall somewhere between the greatest and the least of His, we should serve one another.

Ministry is manifested in three general categories: fellowship, discipleship, and evangelism. Our tendency is to choose which category we like best. But we all are called to practice our love for one another in all three ways.

Fellowship

When you were saved, you were placed into the body of Christ. I don't know about your body, but my body works as a unit. My hand doesn't work without the help of my arm. If I didn't have a torso, what would my legs hang from? My heart can't pump blood throughout my body without veins and arteries. That blood won't be pure without my liver. I can't taste my food without a sense of smell, and I can't walk a straight line because of a little fluid in my ear. Not one body part works independently of all the other parts. All parts follow instructions from my brain. This is fellowship.

Fellowship means interdependence. Fellowship is more than just hanging out with the saints. It is that part of ministry that emphasizes the interdependence between saints. My walk with God is not about just God and me any more than Jesus' life on earth was about just God and Him. We are a world of imperfect people. Fellowship fills in the gaps among us and between us. Fellowship means that if you have cracks, I have putty, and somebody else has paint. Fellowship is your hammer with my nails, his car with her fuel. Fellowship is new math. It's one plus one equals three! Jesus said if one person gets together with another person in His name, He'd be there in the midst to make it a divine threesome.

Fellowship takes maturity. We are the body of Christ, not the bodies of Christ. Paul said the goal is to be so unified by our faith in Jesus that we come together and move as one with His brain giving us directions. Fellowship takes maturity. There are some parts of the body that are more vital than others, but that doesn't matter to the individual parts if the body is healthy. My big toe never wants to be a spleen. It doesn't leave my foot in a huff when it finds out my body can live without it. It's interesting that the most vital parts of our body are unseen. We ought to be willing to be unseen if that is God's desire for us. Everybody's not called to stand up and preach at a pulpit.

You may love God enough to want to shout His glory from the rooftops, but do you love Him enough to give somebody two dollars to catch the bus when nobody's looking? Do you love Him enough to stuff envelopes or baby-sit in children's church? If God has called you to be the heart of your congregation, can you do it without a compliment or a thank-you or even a nod? We usually don't notice our internal organs unless something is wrong with them, and then our response is to complain. Can you do what God has called you to do if all you hear from people are complaints?

Fellowship begins and ends with love. We cannot be in fellowship with one another if we're not even trying to love one another. On a simple level, fellowship is just being part of God's family. Sometimes that means being nice to your brothers and sisters. Some folks go through hell all week long, then come to church and have to sit next to someone who is too mean to say hello. Squeezing a "good morning" out of some people is like drawing blood. A greeting is the beginning of fellowship, not the end. Simple common courtesy is a given in fellowship, not an option.

It breaks my heart when people come to church and feel out of place because someone disapproves of what they're wearing. I have seen women ushered out of church because they were wearing pants. Church folks are playing dress up while people are broken and dying right next to them in the pew.

Man focuses on that junk outside. God tries to find out what's under that silk and satin. What kind of heart do you have? How much love do you have? How much compassion, how much caring?

There is an atmosphere that the Lord moves in. When glory fills the house, it fills it to such a degree that people can't even stand. The glory of the Lord creates an atmosphere. The anointing of God, His power, cannot come through you with all kinds of carnal mess blocking it. God is trying to heal. He's trying to touch and deliver. He's trying to do it through you and me. He's trying to do it through us as a body. How in the world can we say that we love God when we can't even speak to each other?

God is calling us to a another level of association. We are being led to fellowship, which means rejoicing, praying, touching, loving, and affecting one another's lives. It means ministering to one another in a spirit of unity.

Discipleship

General Motors has a product—cars. Xerox has a product—copiers. Discipleship should have its own product—changed lives.

Discipleship is the process of producing godly men and godly women by giving them the example of Christ to follow. Matthew 28:20 commands us to go out and make disciples, "teaching them to observe all things that I [Jesus] have commanded you." Notice we are to teach disciples to observe all things. He didn't say teach them to memorize. He said teach them to observe, which means the effectiveness of our discipleship is incumbent on our disciples' doing what they're taught. That means changing lives.

You can't change lives without telling the truth. If we are to love our neighbors as ourselves, we must minister to them from a place of truth. We have to love them enough to let the example of Christ shine through us lighting the way for them to follow. We have to allow the truth to give them comfort in their pain but yet make them uncomfortable in their sin. We have to be willing to allow the truth to expose the lies in their lives and in our own.

Discipleship does not mean I walk before you perfectly. It means my desire is toward perfection, mine and yours. It means I'm willing to let the Holy Spirit clean me up, for your sake, so that you can see how to do it in your own life. My goal is to lay out a path for you to follow—a path of righteousness when I can help it—and a path of repentance when I can't.

A willing minister exposes all that he is for the sake of his disciples. He exposes his strengths and his weaknesses. If he tells the truth, and he should, his strength is always Christ. Discipleship requires the greatest love, because the success of it depends on the minister's laying down his life for the disciple. Loving people through discipleship means loving them through their mess. It means helping them through struggles you put behind you a long time ago. Sometimes it means revisiting old hurts and reliving past pain for the sake of another.

Then, sometimes it means refusing to comfort someone in his disobedience. Sometimes we have to love someone enough to get out of the way and let God discipline him, if that's what He needs you to do. If a person chooses to jump off a bridge, sometimes God wants you there, not to catch her, but to help pick up the pieces after He allows her to hit bottom.

Discipleship is truth and mercy together. Truth without mercy is condemnation. Mercy without truth is compromise. The former means your destruction. The latter will destroy your disciple.

Evangelism

If you were lost, you'd want somebody to come and get you. Loving your neighbors as yourself means loving them enough to go after them. In Mark 16:15, Jesus said "Go into all the world." In Acts 1:8, He said, "You shall be witnesses to Me in Jerusalem, and in all Judea and Samaria, and to the end of the earth."

Evangelism means going. Godly people go. The church should be full of goers. For many churches the emphasis is placed on coming. Come hear my preacher, come hear my choir, come see our robes, come celebrate our anniversary. Come, come, come. We find comfort in coming.

Going, however, makes us responsible for acting. Most of us would rather be acted upon. We'd rather be held than go hold someone. We'd rather come to class than go teach. But Jesus said, "Go." Peter wanted to build a temple on the Mount of Transfiguration so people could come, but Jesus said, "Go." *Come* is for salvation. Once you have come, all efforts are toward equipping you to go.

My job as a pastor is to prepare you to go. You may ask, "Go where?"

Go out into the world to be witnesses of Christ (Acts 1:8). You should go and make a difference in the world because you are different, and that difference is your relationship with Christ.

Evangelism is ministering light in a dark world. When you love people through evangelism, you serve them and give them the thing they need most: the truth about who Jesus is and who He can be to them. Evangelism is finding God's lost sheep. It is binding up the broken ones and feeding the hungry ones. Evangelism is the purest form of ministry because it requires a heart that loves Jesus enough to tell the truth about Him and loves another enough to bring him home at all cost. There is no place for pride in evangelism, no place for anger, deceit, or covetousness. Effective evangelism is effective fellowship, discipleship, worship, belief, and obedience. It is loving God with all your heart, mind, and soul. It is loving your neighbor as yourself.

Evangelism requires submission to everything but your own will. You must submit to the truth of the knowledge of God. You must submit to the needs of the person to whom you witness and his or her understanding of the truth. Evangelism is committing and submitting yourself completely to the prompting of the Holy Spirit. It is putting everything before yourself or any rights you have claimed for yourself. Getting the most out of evangelism means becoming the least in all areas of your life, except the capacity to be filled with the Spirit.

Evangelism can't be faked. The Spirit of God works in an atmosphere of truth. Evangelism is God's drawing someone to Himself through someone else. God is always doing the drawing. If someone comes to salvation, it is because the Spirit of the Lord moved him or her and moved in each of them. That is not to say people have not witnessed in their flesh, or that people have not come to God out of a false response to pressure or emotionalism. But genuine evangelism leading to genuine salvation can only be accomplished by the truth of God moving in someone's heart. That can only happen when the Spirit of God is present.

One Commandment in Two

Jesus gave us two commandments. He taught us to love the Lord with all our hearts, minds, and souls, and to love our neighbor as ourselves. He continued with the second command, like the first, by teaching there is nothing you will ever face, nothing that will ever challenge you that cannot be dealt with, if you do these two things.

With these two commandments, God set up a cycle of reaction. It begins with Him loving us, which leads us to loving Him and becoming more like Him. Now, as we become more like Him, we love one another. As we love one another, we show God to one another because God is love. As we see love in one another, we behold "as in a mirror the glory of the Lord, are being transformed into the same image from glory to glory" (2 Cor. 3:18). In other words, the more we see God, the godlier we become. When we love the Lord with all our hearts, minds, and souls, we can't help loving one another. This makes us love God more because we see Him in one another.

Jesus talked to the scribes about the Great Commandment.

Prayer
for
Obedience

Lord God, You have given us the keys to the
    kingdom in two commandments.
Give me a heart that is committed to loving You
    completely.
Show me how to love You with my whole heart,
    mind, and soul.
Give me a servant's spirit, so I can minister to
    my brothers and sisters.
Let my life be one of the "glories" You use to
    help transform someone else's life.
Take my right to my own life.
Show me how to lose my life that You might
    live through me.
Commit me to Your service and the service of
    others.
In Jesus' name, Amen.

Chapter 5 Exercises

Exercise 1: The Great Commandment
Memorize Matthew 22:37–39:

> Jesus said to him, "'You shall love the Lord your God with all
> your heart, with all your soul, and with all your mind.' This is the
> first and great commandment. And the second is like it: 'You
> shall love your neighbor as yourself.'"

Loving God is rooted in commitment. It is you committing
yourself to God and God alone. Then God commits Himself to
you, making all that you do possible.

Loving your neighbor is fleshed out in ministry by meeting
the needs of others. This is accomplished through fellowship,
discipleship, and evangelism.

Exercise 2: With All My Heart
David was a man after God's own heart. Most of us take this
to mean that David tried to get into the heart of God. He wanted
to get close to God. I believe that to be accurate. I would suggest
that there is a second, equally true interpretation of that phrase
"a man after God's own heart." In addition to seeking God's
heart, David also wanted to have the heart of God. We read
much in the Psalms about God indicating David had access to
what was in God's heart. But we also learn much in Scripture
about what was in the heart of David himself.

1. Read 1 Samuel 17:45–50. Why was David able to defeat Goliath?

_____

_____

_____

_____

_____

2. Read 1 Kings 9:4 and 11:4–6. How did David's relationship with God differ from his son Solomon's?

_____

_____

_____

_____

_____

3. Read Psalm 29. Now write your own psalm about "the Voice of the Lord."

_____

_____

_____

_____

_____

Exercise 3: With All My Mind

Loving the Lord with all your mind means having a mind that is completely controlled by the Spirit of God. Paul gave us a blueprint in Philippians 2:5–9 for the mind we are to have as children of God:

Let this mind be in you which was also in Christ Jesus, who, being in the form of God, did not consider it robbery to be equal with God, but made Himself of no reputation, taking the form of a bondservant, and coming in the likeness of men. And being found in appearance as a man, He humbled Himself, and became obedient to the point of death, even the death of the cross. Therefore God also has highly exalted Him and given Him the name which is above every name.

Within this text, we see Paul's blueprint for our mind represented in Jesus.

1. Reality: Jesus knew He was God.
2. Circumstance: He was human.
3. Inward response: He humbled Himself.
4. Outward response: Obedience.

Think of a situation where you are required to have the mind of Christ. Break it down to fit the template presented above. Begin with the unseen reality that you are a child of God, holy, saved, and predestined to be conformed to the image of Christ. Then look at your present circumstance. What does God expect your inward response to be, and how will it manifest itself as an outward response? Be specific about the situation and your behavior. I filled in the first blank to get you started.

1. My reality: <u>I am a child of God.</u>
2. My circumstance: _____
3. My inward response: _____
4. My outward response: _____

Notice God's response to Jesus (Phil. 2:9). God never forgets to reward a proper response to Him. A person who seeks to belong completely to God shouldn't be concerned with whether or not God sees him or her when doing His will. This is wasted energy.

Exercise 4: With All My Soul

How do you know that you love the Lord with all your soul? What is your soul? It is that most basic part of you, the part of you that says simply, "I am." So how do you know that "I am" loves the Lord completely? When I stop knowing that "I am," I start knowing that "I am His." When I have lost my life, I know that I will find it again in Him.

Scripture shows us a beautiful illustration of a soul completely in love with God in the life of John the Baptist. The prophets of old heralded his coming (Isa. 40:3; Mal. 4:5–6). Many followed him to Christ even before Christ was in the flesh. Jesus spoke of him in Luke 7:28: "Among those born of women there is not a greater prophet than John the Baptist." He lived and died with the singular obsession to carry out the will of God. John the Baptist's life is one worth studying for its lessons in focus, determination, loyalty, submission, leadership, and obedience, among other things. Read Mark 1:1–8, Matthew 3:13–17, John 3:22–30, and Matthew 14:1–12, in that order. This condensed account of his life challenges us to examine our own devotion to God.

Self-examination

1. Have you ever been angry or disappointed because you didn't get credit for your work on a job, at home, or at your church?
2. Do you sometimes get distracted from your work by personal issues or conflicts with others?

3. Has your pride ever negatively affected your work?
4. Do you sometimes find it difficult to lead others?
5. Do you sometimes find it difficult to follow others?
6. Have you ever lied to save face?
7. Have you ever let other people's opinion of you affect your work?

Chapter 6
The Conflict of Godliness

Blessed is he whose transgression is forgiven,
Whose sin is covered.
Blessed is the man to whom the LORD does not impute
iniquity,
And in whose spirit there is no deceit.

When I kept silent, my bones grew old
Through my groaning all the day long.
For day and night Your hand was heavy upon me;
My vitality was turned into the drought of summer.
I acknowledged my sin to You,
And my iniquity I have not hidden.
I said, "I will confess my transgressions to the LORD,"
And You forgave the iniquity of my sin.

For this cause everyone who is godly shall pray to You
In a time when You may be found;
Surely in a flood of great waters
They shall not come near him.

Psalm 32:1–6

"For this cause everyone who is godly shall pray to You."
What shall they pray for? Forgiveness. Everyone who is
godly needs to seek forgiveness because sin is in conflict with
godliness. Sin is making a choice to do that which is contrary to
the Word, will, and way of God.

But even godly people sin. Paul said God is still working on us, and He won't be finished until Jesus comes back (Phil. 1:6). Jeremiah said God gives us new mercies every morning (Lam. 3:22–23). If we were perfect, we wouldn't require mercy. Godliness is not about perfection. This message is deliverance for someone who thinks godliness means "sinlessness."

Paul said the Spirit wars with your flesh (Gal. 5:17), so that even saved folks have a hard time doing what they ought to do (Rom. 7:19). In case you didn't know it, struggling with sin is a standard issue in your salvation kit. John said God is faithful to forgive our sins. John explained about the sins that believers commit (1 John 1:9). What then separates the godly from everybody else? How can we be in the world, but not of the world, if we sin just like the world?

One of the keys to living a life of godliness is the understanding that the line of demarcation between the godly and the ungodly is not one of action, but of attitude. Godliness does not speak of one's perfection regarding sin. It speaks of one's perception. The Bible says all have sinned, but godly men and women see sin from God's perspective. Remember, walking with God means commitment. And commitment, as we learned earlier, implies agreement, not conflict. If our goal is godliness, we agree to recognize sin as God does, regard it as He does, and respond to it as He would respond. First, though, we must agree with God's basic definition of sin.

The Concept of Sin

King David, the composer of Psalm 32, is arguably one of the greatest sovereigns in the history of the nation of Israel. As an anointed writer, he is one of the greatest sages in all of Scripture. As a man after God's own heart, he is one of the greatest saints in all of Scripture. And yet, a careful examination of his life reveals that he was also one of the greatest sinners in all of Scripture. Chief among his transgressions was an adulterous affair with a woman named Bathsheba.

Look very carefully in your Bible at the title of Psalm 32. Under it there is a subheading that labels this psalm a Maschil. The word *maschil* is a Hebrew word that means "to make understood, to instruct or to teach." Psalm 32 is one of fifteen *maschils* that were to be sung, not only for praise and thanksgiving, but also as tools of teaching. It is believed that Psalm 32 was meant to chronologically follow Psalm 51, David's Psalm of Repentance, following his confrontation with the prophet Nathan about his sin with Bathsheba. The Bible says that when Nathan showed him his sin, David immediately confessed and quickly repented. He recorded his repentance in Psalm 51:

Have mercy upon me, O God,
According to Your lovingkindness;
According to the multitude of Your tender mercies,
Blot out my transgressions.
Wash me thoroughly from my iniquity,
And cleanse me from my sin . . .

Create in me a clean heart, O God,
And renew a steadfast spirit within me . . .

Then I will teach transgressors Your ways,
And sinners shall be converted to You. (Ps. 51:1–2, 10, 13)

David repented, then made a promise to God. He said in effect, "Lord, when you forgive me and cleanse me, I will teach others how to deal with sin the way you had me deal with it."

In Psalm 32 David kept the promise he made in Psalm 51. The purpose of the psalm is to teach. Verse 6 tells us who the students are: "For this cause everyone who is godly shall pray to You / In a time when you may be found." Psalm 32 was written to teach those who would be godly something about their relationship with God.

It also presents a vivid picture of ungodliness that goes beyond a simple act of evil or unkindness. Look at verses 1 and 2: "Blessed is he whose transgression is forgiven, / Whose sin is covered. / Blessed is the man to whom the Lord does not impute iniquity, / And in whose spirit there is no deceit."

Transgression, sin, iniquity, and *deceit.* These terms are similar in that they refer to things that are all hated by God and are an affront to the holy nature of Him. We have been released from the bondage of each of them by Christ's sacrifice on the cross. But these four words, though related, are not synonymous. In penning Psalm 32 David was not redundant. He was, in fact, thorough, leaving us no room for uncertainty regarding the form of evil that we are to avoid or the singularity and sufficiency of God to extinguish it in us.

Transgression. Transgression is rebellion. It is a revolt against the authority of God in our lives. Transgression is the picture of a parent telling a child to do something and that child replying, "No!" What you need to see is that transgression is blatant. It's neither deaf nor blind. When a child rebels against a parent, nobody's confused about who is the parent and who is the child. Transgression makes a choice to ignore the authority of the one in charge. Transgression breaks God's heart because it knows who God is—it just doesn't care.

Not only does transgression presuppose knowledge of who is in authority, it also presupposes understanding of the rules put forth by that authority. To transgress means "to go beyond known set limits." David was a priest, which meant he spoke to God on the people's behalf. He was a prophet, which meant he spoke to the people on God's behalf. He knew God, and he knew God's commandments. In his sin with Bathsheba, he made a choice to ignore them both.

The most significant component of transgression is premeditation. It's not just rebellion, but planned rebellion. It's making an appointment to defy God and putting it in your mental day planner. It's knowing ahead of time that what you're going to do is wrong and deciding to do it anyway. Now don't limit your thinking to such obvious transgressions as an illicit rendezvous or a premeditated crime. When was the last time you picked up the phone to confirm or spread some gossip? Have you ever been undercharged for something and left the store without telling the salesperson? Are you already planning to write off some items on your taxes that you know you're not really entitled to?

Sin. If you take away the premeditative element of transgression, you're left with sin. Sin is turning away from the authority of God or going off track. It is the picture of someone trying to hit a specific target, but missing the mark. He falls short. Like transgression, sin understands the authority of God and His commands. But where transgression is rooted in prideful self-fulfillment, sin is rooted in a lack of self-control and dull spiritual senses. It is failure in the sense that a person may have tried to do the right thing or at least wanted to, but still did not.

Iniquity. Iniquity comes from the Hebrew root word that means "bent" or "crooked." It speaks of a crooked or perverted character flaw. It is one's natural bent or tendency toward sin. Picture a marksman with a rifle. Transgression is deliberately shooting into the air. Sin is aiming at a target, but missing it. Iniquity is a gun with a crooked sight. No matter how well you line it up with the target, barring some outside adjustment, you're predisposed to miss it. The Bible says that because of Adam's sin, we are born crooked and out of right relationship with God.

Deceit. Do you want to get depressed? Ask God to show you the deceit, or insincerity, in your heart. It is an attempt to hide the truth from God or another person through deception. Deceit is a wrong motive that looks like right behavior. It's smiling and saying good morning to someone you know doesn't like you, not because you really want them to have a good morning, but because you know it irritates them to see you happy. It's using the Word of God to prove yourself right, instead of using it to prove the righteousness of God. It is harboring unconfessed sin, yet operating as though you are in right relationship with God.

Like transgression, deceit is deliberate and finds its source in pride. Like sin, it is a turning away from God. Of course, it is nurtured by our iniquity or natural bent toward sin. But the aim of deceit is to set out to distort the truth. Transgression, sin, and iniquity—all of these defy God. Deceit betrays Him. God is truth, and deceit attempts to twist truth into something else.

Recognizing Sin

Crucial to godliness is the ability to recognize sin as God does. The meaning of recognition here goes beyond the idea of perceiving something that was previously known. That may be a process we have to go through now and again, but God never has to "realize" that sin is sin because He already knows everything. Rather, we must recognize sin in the sense of acknowledgment, which is "to admit knowledge of or agreement with a fact." In other words, it is recognizing sin by calling it just that, sin. God doesn't call sin anything but sin. We, on the other hand, call it everything but sin. We make mistakes. We tell little white lies. We have weaknesses, needs, tendencies, and issues. We are subject to our orientation, preferences, and predisposition. We say we are only human, and therefore fallible. We can't help ourselves.

These are our attempts to lay hold of what Dietrich Bonhoeffer called "cheap grace"—the proclamation of forgiveness without the requirement of repentance. It is assuming that as long as I do godly things, I am in good standing with God. So I don't mention my sin. It is seeking the power of God, the anointing of God, the face of God, and the prosperity of God, without dealing with the holy nature of God.

David tried to live on cheap grace. If you clock the chronology of his story, you would discover that a year lapsed between David's sin with Bathsheba and his confrontation with Nathan about it. David, the great anointed king, priest, and prophet, stood before God and his people for over a year without confessing his sin. The Scripture says he "kept silence." We can logically assume that during that year he asked God to bless him and his people. We can assume that during that year he brought sacrificial offerings unto God. We can even assume that during that year he brought word to the people from God. David remained in the face of God trying to keep a secret. How do you keep a secret from an omniscient God? How, indeed, do you hide when in His omnipresence He was with your secret before it came to be with you?

David did what many of us try to do today. He didn't mention his sin. To keep others from mentioning it, he tried to make his sin look legitimate. He waited for Bathsheba to mourn her dead husband, dead by David's hand, then he took her as his wife. She even bore him a son. From all appearances, God had blessed him. But Scripture says God was not pleased. How familiar is that to many of us. God blesses us, despite our sin. We sin, despite God's blessings.

Sometimes—more than I care to admit—I have to discipline my son Kendan. And every once in awhile, he'll say, "Daddy, just this once, could you let me slide?" And every once in awhile I do because I start to think about the times when God let me slide. God let David slide for over a year, and then He sent Nathan to tell Him: "Dave, you messed up. God knows you messed up, and He ain't happy."

It's at this point that we see one of the reasons why David is called a man after God's own heart. When Nathan confronted David with his sin, he didn't make any excuses. He didn't try to justify, lie, or analyze his way out of it. He didn't say, "Look, I know it started out wrong, but I fixed it up. I made it legal. I brought it up to God's standard." He heard what God said about what he had done, and he quickly agreed with God. Nathan said, "You blew it" and David's response was, "You're right. I blew it."

Recognizing sin as God does means recognizing it immediately, not necessarily with respect to the occurrence of the sin, but with respect to the revelation of it. When God shows us sin, He's not asking us to confirm it. He's asking us to confess it. The Greek word for *confess* is interesting. It is the word *homologeo*. This is a compound word. The root is the word *logeo* from the verb meaning "to say." The prefix is *homo*, which means "the same" or "the same thing." Put them together and you have the idea behind confess. It means "to say the same thing." When I confess my sin, I say what God says about what I did. I call what I did the same thing God calls it. In other words, when God says you blew it, all He's looking to hear is: "Yes, Lord. I blew it."

Regarding Sin

To regard sin as God does is to have the same opinion about it as He has. Regard goes beyond perception to perspective. Where recognition is mental, regard is emotional. The focus is not on what we see, but on how we feel about what we see. Regard is that necessary bridge between recognition and response. It is born from the former and gives birth to the latter.

Identifying sin in our lives is useless if we don't have a proper regard for it. And how we regard sin is crucial to how, or if, we respond to it. In that war fought between flesh and spirit, our regard for sin serves as the battleground. Truth wins or loses here. Recognition is validated or violated by our regard. Response is produced, perverted, or aborted by it.

In Satan's perfect world you would never recognize sin. It would never be revealed to you. It would remain in darkness where he could, through sin, continue to exercise his God-given control over you. Still, Satan is not that worried about your recognizing sin if it doesn't bother you. Regard requires a heart response. Those who would be godly must have a heart that is consistent with God's when it comes to the things of this world and sin in particular. These are defensible by His Word.

Sin Belongs to Us

In Psalm 51:5 we read: "Behold, I was brought forth in iniquity, / And in sin my mother conceived me." David understood that his sin began and ended with him. As sons of Adam, we are born into sin. Our nature is sinful. We come into this world at enmity with God (Rom. 5:12). It's important that we take ownership of our sin. It seems easy, even reasonable, sometimes to look outside ourselves, to justify ourselves. But the sufficiency of Christ to conquer sin in us would be invalidated if the source or cause of our sin lay beyond us. If something or someone could make you sin, or if your sin didn't find its origin in you, your deliverance from it would be tied to something or someone extraneous to you and Christ.

Ironically, it is this proprietary sensibility toward sin that keeps us from being overwhelmed by the fact of sin in our lives. Knowing that sin is a part of us keeps us ever mindful of God's mercy. He loved us before the world was formed, knowing who we would be, knowing we would sin.

Understanding our sinful nature also keeps us from being abused by it. If you're struggling when you see sin in your life, you're struggling with the wrong thing. This is akin to the snake struggling with its poison. It is misdirected energy. A common ploy of the devil is to get you to expend your energy on the wrong thing.

Settle this: If a particular area of sin has been brought to your attention, Satan did not bring it. Satan was given dominion over darkness, and that's where he wants to keep your sin. The Holy Spirit operates in light by a process of revelation. If you can see your sin, God is the one showing it to you. However, once you see it, Satan works real hard to put a spin on what you see. He'll tell you you're not good enough to be God's child if you're still wrestling with this or that. He'll make you wonder if you'll be rejected when others find out about your stuff. He may even try to convince you that what you see is not really sin or that God understands and excuses it. His goal is to make you ashamed enough to hide your sin, afraid enough to hide from it, or arrogant enough to ignore it. In any case, you will have put it back in darkness and, therefore, under Satan's control. Regarding sin as ours keeps it out of Satan's reach.

Sin Is Harmful to Us

In Psalm 32:3–4 we read: "When I kept silent, my bones grew

old / Through my groaning all the day long. . . / My vitality was turned into the drought of summer."

These are the same bones David referred to in Psalm 51:8 when he said, "Make me hear joy and gladness, / That the bones You have broken may rejoice." This is an interesting picture of the effects of unconfessed sin. David said his bones "grew old." That means they started to decay. Your skeleton houses and supports your entire body. A person's bones are symbolic of the framework of his life. David's vitality was turned into the drought of summer. One Bible translation says "my sap has been drained." It is the idea of a plant that's dying because its life has been drained by the scorching heat in the midst of a summer.

In Scripture, dry places are always indicative of the absence of God. God is most often associated with vitality, water springing up (John 4:14), refreshing rain (Ps. 68:9), mighty streams (Amos 5:24), and rivers (Isa. 32:2). Without Him, we're in a spiritual drought, parched, weak, and thirsty.

Here's the picture so far. David kept silent about his sin. His life became a desert without the refreshing, life-giving force of God's Spirit flowing through him. Life is hard-pressed to flourish in a desert.

When bones are dry, they become brittle and easily broken. Notice in Psalm 51:8 David referred to "the bones You have broken." He said the Lord had broken his bones. How? Look at Psalm 32:4: "Day and night Your hand was heavy upon me." The heavy hand David talked about was the pressure he felt in his spirit from the weight of his guilt. This depicts the image of being held down by something stronger than you are. In this case, it was God's judgment. When we sin, we place ourselves under His hand of judgment. If we confess immediately, the pressure is lifted. If we hold on to sin because of fear, shame, or pride, the pressure remains. The more we try to get out from under it by making excuses, covering up, or denying sin, the weaker we become. You see, God will never help keep you in sin. So all your efforts to hold on to it or hide from it are carried out in your own strength, which eventually runs out. Without strength, you can no longer remain under the pressure of the guilt of your sin, so your bones, which are already dry, are easily broken.

Sin Is Bigger Than We Are

In Psalm 51:1 we read: "Have mercy upon me, O God, / According to Your lovingkindness."

Sin is not only harmful, it is stronger than we are. In our own power, we cannot control it (Rom. 7:18–20), and if sin is left unchecked, it ultimately will destroy us (Prov. 21:15; Isa. 1:28). God knows the damaging and sometimes deadly effects of sin. He won't allow it to kill us spiritually, but He will allow it to break us. After David confessed his sin, God said in Psalm 32:9, "Do not be like the horse or like the mule, / Which have no understanding, / Which must be harnessed with bit and bridle, / Else they will not come near you." He said for us not to be like a horse or a mule because to yield to either instinct will get us into spiritual trouble.

Of course, God would have to warn us about that because He knows we have horse and mule tendencies. The way you end up in sin in the first place is by following, at some point, your horse or mule sense. The tendency of a horse is to run and run and run, which is a lack of self-control. The tendency of a mule is to not move at all, which is stubbornness. Both horses and mules act on their own with no understanding, which is why they have to be controlled by the bit and the bridle.

The bridle is fitted over the head of an animal and is attached to reins. The bit is an instrument, usually metal, placed in the mouth of the animal. As long as the animal moves according to the prompting of the master, everything is fine. As soon as the horse or mule resists, the reins of the bridle are pulled. This, in turn, pulls on the bit putting painful pressure on the roof of the animal's mouth, which will make an animal do just about anything you want it to.

Remember the Lone Ranger's horse, Silver? That animal was so smart it was scary. All the Lone Ranger had to do was say, "Hi-yo, Silver!" and the horse listened. You never saw the Lone Ranger beating up on Silver or yanking on the reins. Whatever he told him to do, the horse did it. Silver obeyed the voice of his master. Sometimes you'd see the Lone Ranger shooting at the bad guys with a gun in each hand. He didn't even have to hold on to Silver. Silver knew exactly what to do. That's godliness. Godliness is when you obey the voice of God without Him having to make you obey.

Here's the catch. If you came in and saw some of the latter segments of *The Lone Ranger*, you would assume that Silver had always been that smart. But if you go back to the first episode, you'd find out this wasn't so. The Lone Ranger started off as a Texas Ranger who survived a massacre and was left for dead. In a canyon he found a great white, wild stallion. There were several scenes of the Lone Ranger riding Silver. When he began, Silver was jumping and bucking, bucking and jumping. The Lone Ranger kept riding him. Silver kept jumping. The Lone Ranger kept riding. It's like Silver was saying, "How long are we going to do this, brother?" The Lone Ranger replied, "How long are you going to fight me?"

Finally, Silver pranced. When the Lone Ranger said, "turn left," Silver turned left. When he said, "turn right," Silver turned right. The Lone Ranger had to break Silver of his tendency to move according to his own will. Once Silver was broken, the Lone Ranger could use him.

God loves you so much that He's going to ride you until He breaks you. He's not going to get off your back. He's not going to give up on you. He loves you just the way you are, but He loves you too much to leave you the way you are. He's going to stay on your back until you are broken and you can say, "Now Lord, what do you want me to do right now?"

Don't underestimate the power of sin. But also don't underestimate God's power over sin waiting at your disposal. Be grateful when He tries to tame you.

Jesus Understands Sin

In Hebrews 4:15 we read: "For we do not have a High Priest who cannot sympathize with our weaknesses, but was in all points tempted as we are, yet without sin."

The function of a priest is to stand before God on behalf of the people. The Bible says Jesus the Christ is our high priest. He stands before God on our behalf. The Bible also says we must understand that Jesus is not the kind of high priest who cannot be touched with the feeling of our infirmity. This means He is not someone who cannot relate to where you're coming from or what you're going through. He was "at all points tempted as we are, yet without sin." Don't miss that. There is not a temptation that you will ever face that Jesus has not already faced. That's too deep for most of us.

One of the reasons that we don't confess certain kinds of sin is because we have an erroneous concept that they are insignificant to God. Or we think that He understands that we are fragile and forgives us without our asking. Or we think He can't relate, so why go to Him? The Bible says He understands because He has been tempted just like we are.

Sometimes, as parents, we tell our children that they can tell us anything. We want them to understand that whatever they're going through, for the most part, we have been there, done that, gotten the T-shirt and the hat. Jesus says He's been there too. He knows how you feel. He knows life's hard. It was hard for Him. He knows you're struggling. He struggled. That means, brother, if a woman tempts you, Jesus can relate. That means, sister, if a man tempts you, Jesus can relate. You have to understand that—otherwise, you will conclude that He can't help you because He can't comprehend what you're going through. Then you'll never go to Him.

Responding to Sin

If the world were one big school playground, we'd be the little guys with the horn-rimmed glasses and the pencil protectors, and sin would be the class bully. He picks on us all the time. We've been called out, talked about, and tracked down by him. When he catches us, he beats us up. Some of us get caught more often than we should. We run too slowly, or we don't run until it's too late. Others would rather switch than fight. We give him our lunch money and anything else he asks for. We try to become friends with him to keep him from beating us up.

But if we're smart, we're always on the lookout for sin. We have already determined where he hangs out, and we avoid those places. We know every shortcut home. We seek safety in fellowship with others. If preventive action fails, and we find ourselves face to face with our enemy, we run. We do not wonder how he caught up with us or spend time in conversation with him. We do not walk. We run. Once we see sin and understand it as something destructive and more powerful than we are, our response to it should be whatever it takes to put the most distance between it and us.

The purpose of running, however, is not to get away. If we run long enough, sin will always outrun us. Remember that sin is bigger and stronger than we are. No, the purpose of running is not to *get away* so much as it is to *get to*. Everybody's got that person he can run to when a bully is after him, somebody bigger and stronger than the bully. He's that person who sees you coming, puts his arms around you, feels your fear, and wipes your tears. He's that friend who says, "Where is he? I'll take care of him," then springs into action.

For some, it's a brother; for others, it's a father. There are more than a few protective mothers out there. But for the child of God, that Protector, that Big Brother is the Holy Ghost. Throughout Scripture, God is seen protecting, guiding, and providing for His people by His Spirit. The breath of God is His Spirit. The power of His Word is His Spirit. The force of His hand, the beat of His heart, and His mercy and grace toward us—these things are His Spirit. It is that Spirit we call upon to defeat sin in our lives.

The godly way to respond to sin is by letting God respond to it—by looking to Him for protection and direction. Notice how David began Psalm 51 crying out for the Lord to cleanse him from his sin. He finished with a desire to please God. A godly response to sin begins and ends with God.

This is not to say we have no work to do. This process of dealing with sin is interactive. First of all, once God has brought sin to our attention, we have to confess it. In other words, we have to agree with Him that we have sinned. This is active on our part, and it is God's way of putting us back in right relationship with Him, in agreement with Him. Without confession, we are in disagreement with Him and, therefore, opposed to Him. Secondly, once we confess our sin, we must repent of it. This is the picture of turning from sin to go in the opposite direction. It is denouncing what you have confessed as sin. Thirdly, we must follow God's direction in eliminating that sin in us. Confession and repentance don't necessarily guarantee that the tendency to commit a specific sin is gone. Often it is not. But when we obey the constraint of the Holy Spirit, we walk in the truth of our deliverance. Every act of obedience prepares us for another act of obedience. Eventually that sin loses its hold. Lastly, when God delivers us from sin, we are expected, encouraged, and empowered to deliver others. Like David, we are to teach others how to live godly lives.

So we should respond to sin by going to God, acknowledging our sin to Him, and letting Him cleanse us. In Psalm 32:5, David said, "I acknowledged my sin to You, / And my iniquity I have not hidden. / I said, 'I will confess my transgressions to the LORD,' / And You forgave the iniquity of my sin." In other words, he said, "I will confess my sin, and He will forgive me." The text implies an immediacy of forgiveness. When David sincerely repented, with no deceit, when he was sincerely broken about his sin, when he came before God with a contrite heart, God immediately forgave him.

It is almost amazing how it happens. When you come to God, sincere and repentant, you don't have to bargain with Him for your forgiveness. You don't have to negotiate with Him. He and Jesus struck a deal about your sin before the world was formed (Acts 2:23). He is always ready to respond.

God's Response to Our Response

In Hebrews 4:16 we read: "Let us therefore come boldly to the throne of grace, that we may obtain mercy and find grace to help in time of need."

The beautiful thing about sincere repentance is that God always responds. He knows exactly what you need. When you sin, you need two things: mercy and grace. Grace is when God gives you something you don't deserve. When you sin, you don't deserve to be blessed. So, whatever blessing you get after you sin is grace. You don't have to go deep to find a blessing. The very fact that He still allows you to breathe His air after you defiled Him with your sin shows you've already received some grace. The air that He gave you was air that you didn't deserve. Whenever He gives you something that you don't deserve, that's grace. Now, when He doesn't give you what you do deserve, that's mercy. If you're reading this, you have received mercy, because all have sinned and the wages of sin is death. But you're not dead.

When you sin, God says you can come boldly to His throne to get a helping of mercy and grace. Boldly does not mean arrogantly; you do not go to God and demand His forgiveness. Boldly means "persistently." You go to God with the idea that you will let nothing stop you from getting to Him. It means you understand that you have broken God's law and, therefore, you have broken His heart. But you go in spite of that. In fact, you know that you must go to Him because He is the only One who can handle the sin. You go determined to make things right with Him, falling on your knees before Him, and repenting and sincerely asking Him to forgive. True to His word, He forgives.

To help us more fully understand what He does for us, God has given us vivid images in His Word that depict the different facets of His forgiveness.

God Puts Away Our Sin

In Psalm 32:1 we read: "Blessed is he whose transgression is forgiven."

The word *forgiven* means "taken away." There is an incredible image in Scripture of how God takes away our sin. God actually removes it from the premises. There is a prophetic word given by Zechariah that paints the exact etymological picture represented by this word: "Then the angel who talked with me came out and said to me, 'Lift your eyes now, and see what this is that goes forth.' So I asked, 'What is it?' And he said, 'It is a basket that is going forth.' He also said, 'This is their resemblance throughout the earth'" (Zech. 5:5–6).

Verse 5 says "Lift your eyes now, and see what this is that goes forth." In other words, "Check it out. There's something up in the sky." He says, "It's a basket."

"'Here is a lead disc lifted up, and this is a woman sitting inside the basket'; then he said, 'This is Wickedness!' And he thrust her down into the basket, and threw the lead cover over its mouth" (Zech. 5:7–8).

Get the scene? There's a basket with a heavy lead cover over it. The angel took off the cover to reveal a woman sitting inside. He declared, "This is Wickedness" and put her back down in the basket and put the top back on. Wickedness, or sin, was placed in a basket and covered with a lead top.

> Then I raised my eyes and looked, and there were two women, coming with the wind in their wings; for they had wings like the wings of a stork, and they lifted up the basket between earth and heaven.
>
> So I said to the angel who talked with me, "Where are they carrying the basket?"
>
> And he said to me, "To build a house for it in the land of Shinar; when it is ready, the basket will be set there on its base." (Zech. 5:9–11)

The angel said the two women were taking the basket containing Wickedness to Shinar, where she would be set on her own pedestal. Shinar represented a place that was considered to be off the map, a desolate place removed from civilization. In other words, Wickedness was carried away from their sight. The implication is "away from their remembrance."

God says here's what happens to sin. When you come before the throne of God with boldness, determined to get right with Him, and you confess your sin sincerely with a contrite heart, God takes that sin and puts it in a basket. Then He covers it up with something very heavy so that it stays in the basket. He then dispatches angels to take it off to oblivion, never to be seen, heard, or spoken of again.

God Covers Our Sin

In Psalm 32:1 we read: "Blessed is he whose transgression is forgiven, / Whose sin is covered."

When I respond to my sin in a godly way, God covers it. Covering sin is hiding it; it is the picture of laying hands on it. It's symbolic of what happens when a sacrifice is brought to the altar. The priest lays his hand on the animal's head and covers its head. God says when you confess your sin, He covers your sin with His hand. When He covers it, it cannot be seen anymore. If it cannot be seen, you should not feel guilty about it. Any remnant of guilt that you feel is an attack of the enemy. He tells you that when God said your sin was covered, He lied. Scripture says God cannot lie. When you feel guilty about a sin for which you have sincerely repented, you actually call God a liar. You say, "God didn't cover my sin. He didn't take it away. My sin is still here. I know it is because my guilt is still here."

This is the enemy trying to get you to doubt and distrust God. If he can get you to distrust Him about this one, it'll be easier to get you to distrust Him about the next sin, and so on. Before you know it, you're living a life seeking cheap grace, asking God to forgive you without ever really repenting.

God Pays Our Account

In Psalm 32:2 we read: "Blessed is the man to whom the Lord does not impute iniquity, / And in whose spirit there is no deceit."

God takes away our sin. He covers our sin. He also speaks as a bookkeeper, promising not to impute our iniquity to us, meaning He doesn't put our sin on our account. Blessed is the man whose sin is not on the books.

When I was a little boy, there was a little grocery store about two or three blocks from my house owned by a nice couple, Mr. and Mrs. Margulie. They had this store (which I called "Magoolie's") set up with a great big ledger. In it were the names of everybody in the neighborhood. Everybody had his own page. Sometimes my mother would go to Margulie's, get what she needed, and tell Mr. Margulie to put it on her bill. He'd open that great big book, turn to the page that had our name on it, and record what Mama had bought. Every once in awhile, Mama would send me to Magoolie's for something and tell me to put it on our bill. Now, I never paid the bill that was on the books. I just kept charging stuff. As I got older, I realized that Daddy had paid the bill. By the time I got ready to charge the next piece of bologna, the first piece of bologna had already been paid for. The books were clean, because my daddy had already paid for everything I charged.

God said blessed is he who went down to Mr. Margulie's store. When he got there, his books were clean because Daddy had already paid the bill. He did not have to pay his account, because it had already been paid. God said that when you come before Him and you sincerely repent, the record of that sin is paid for in full. There is no record of your past bill.

God Protects Us from Being Overtaken

In Psalm 32: 5–6 we read:

I acknowledged my sin to You,
And my iniquity I have not hidden.
I said, "I will confess my transgressions to the LORD,"
And You forgave the iniquity of my sin.

For this cause everyone who is godly shall pray to You
In a time when You may be found;
Surely in a flood of great waters
They shall not come near him.

The godly man and the godly woman who with sincere repentance confess their sin before the Lord cannot be overtaken by trials that might flood their lives. Calm, flowing, cleansing waters are associated with God. Floods and other natural disasters are most often imagery for trouble and tribulation. The Word says that for the one who is godly, God becomes a flood stopper.

I was in Port Arthur, Texas, doing a workshop one year. It was raining, day in and day out. It would not stop. Eventually, a flood warning went out in what was called the Golden Triangle, which comprised the cities of Orange, Beaumont, and Port Arthur. People evacuated their homes in certain areas of the city. The rain continued coming down steadily for several days. I was staying at the home of some friends who were told to evacuate. I was ready to hit the road. But my friends said we were up high enough to be safe from the flood. The only precaution they took was to move their furniture out of the front room. And the rain kept falling.

One of the most helpless and most frightening feelings I've ever had was being in the midst of that flood. I tell you, when the water started rising, there were folks all up and down the block praying, humming, singing, having prayer meetings. In the middle of the day, in the middle of the week, in the middle of the street, we were having church! From the front yard we watched the waters roll down the street. Then the water jumped the curb and came into the front yard. We moved to the porch and watched the water flow toward us. Soon, it rose past the yard and up to the porch, so we stood in the doorway and watched as the water crept up the steps of the porch. The saints of God were on the inside praying. It was the most amazing thing I had ever seen in my life. The water came right up to the front door of the front room, splashed under the door just inside the room and stopped. Then it began to subside. We stood there, some of us with tears in our eyes, as we watched that water turn around and go right back out of the house.

As you live a godly life, the rains may come. There cannot be a flood without the rain. There is the assumption of rain. There is the assumption of trials. There is the assumption of tribulation. There is the assumption of trouble. Nowhere in the Bible does it say that when you commit yourself to godliness, you will escape the rain. There is no rain exclusion clause in your salvation contract. But God says if you stay in a constant posture of confession and repentance, if you maintain a right relationship with Him, the waters that rage in your life will only be allowed to rage to a point. They'll only get so close to the child of God before He says stop. God will say, "That's far enough. Go no further. That house is covered. Stop. That son or daughter is covered. Stop. That career is covered. Stop. That marriage is covered. Stop."

God sets the boundaries, and He enforces them. God is a God of the flood who rides on the floods and tells them when to surge and when to cease.

God Becomes Our Hiding Place

In Psalm 32: 6–7 we read:

> For this cause everyone who is godly shall pray to You
> In a time when You may be found;
> Surely in a flood of great waters
> They shall not come near him.
>
> You are my hiding place;
> You shall preserve me from trouble;
> You shall surround me with songs of deliverance.

When I was a kid, we didn't have all these electronic computer games they have now. As a matter of fact, we didn't need any electricity at all to play. Because of this, my son, Kendan, is convinced that I had absolutely no fun as a child. But I did.

We usually played games where somebody was "It," such as hide-and-seek. Whoever "It" was would go to a tree or a wall and cover his face and say, "Last night and the night before, twenty-four robbers came knocking at my door. So I got up, to let them in, and hit them on the head with a rolling pin. Five, ten, fifteen, twenty, twenty-five, thirty, thirty-five . . . Ready or not, here I come!"

While he counted, everyone would run and find a hiding place because when he was finished, he'd come looking for you. If he found you, you had to beat him back to his post, or you were out of the game. So the goal of hide-and-seek was to find the best hiding place from the person who was "It" or be able to outrun "It" to home base. My cousin and I had the best hiding place. There was a hole under Miss Eula Mae's porch. No one could see us, but we could look out through the lattice and see everything. The fun was watching "It" run all over the place trying to find us. Everywhere "It" looked, "It" couldn't find us because we had a safe hiding place.

God said when you come before Him in repentance, He becomes your hiding place. When the devil says, "Ready or not, here I come," you don't have to worry because God already has you hidden. The devil can't see you. You're underneath Miss Eula Mae's porch, safe in His arms. You can see him looking for you in all the places you used to hide yourself. He's looking for you in discouragement, but you're hiding in joy. He's looking for you in heartache, but you're hiding in peace. He's looking for you in anger and bitterness, but you're hiding in meekness and longsuffering. He's looking for you in weariness, but you're hiding in Jesus. Hallelujah!

I came home one day looking for Kendan, but I couldn't find him. He came to my office about ten minutes later. When I asked him where he had been, he said, "Daddy, I was hiding from you." He was so well hidden that I had stopped looking for him.

If you stay hidden in the arms of Jesus and put your trust in Him—if you stay there long enough—there are some things Satan will stop throwing at you. He'll stop looking for you and go mess with somebody else, somebody who has not been delivered.

One day Kendan was hiding from me and had taken his headset into the hiding place with him. He hid for so long that, again, I stopped looking for him. But this time when he came out of his hiding place, he was dancing—dancing to some music I couldn't even hear.

If you stay in God's hiding place long enough and hold onto His hand, He'll give you a song that no one else can hear. You'll start dancing right where you are. David said that God will surround you with songs of deliverance.

Prayer
for
a Godly Perspective

Merciful Father, first I want to thank You for
Jesus, whose death saved my sinful soul.
I know I would have no hope of eternity
without His sacrifice.
Bless You, Savior.
Lord, give me Your eyes, that I might see sin as
You do.
Give me Your heart, that I might despise sin as
You do.
Give me Your wisdom, courage, and faith, that
I might move as You would against sin in
my life.
Father, shine Your light on the dark places in
me.
Expose my heart to me and wash away its
uncleanness. Then, Lord, be my comfort,
my shield, and my hiding place.
And above all, give me the joy of a life's rest in
Your loving arms.
In Jesus' name, Amen.

Chapter 6 Exercises

Exercise 1: My Sin Is Covered
  1. Memorize Psalm 32:1–2:

Blessed is he whose transgression is forgiven,
Whose sin is covered.
Blessed is the man to whom the LORD does not impute iniquity,
And in whose spirit there is no deceit.

2. It is important to remember that godliness is not sinlessness. Look up these Scriptures.

- We are a work in progress.   Philippians 1:6
- We need mercy every day.   Lamentations 3:22–23
- We struggle with sin.   Galatians 5:17
- We all struggle with sin.   1 John 1:8–10

3. Sin as described by David in Psalm 32 is a multi-dimensional concept that is more complex than a simple act of evil or unkindness. Consider the following:

- Transgression: Rebellion against God
- Sin: Turning away from God
- Iniquity: A bent or crookedness toward sin
- Deceit: Insincerity or guile

Exercise 2: A New Vocabulary
Sometimes we try to lessen the impact of sin in our lives by labeling it with softer terms. Sometimes this practice is uninten-

tional. Other times it is an attempt to justify ourselves to others or hide from God. Regardless of our intent, the Holy Spirit is hindered by any attempt at deception. Think about some past behaviors that you intentionally or unintentionally labeled something other than sin.

I made a mistake when I . . .

_____

_____

In a moment of weakness I . . .

_____

_____

I bent the truth a little when I . . .

_____

_____

I couldn't help it when I . . .

_____

_____

Now, revisit these sins and reiterate them by saying "I sinned when I . . ."

Have you ever agreed with God by admitting that you did, in fact, sin? If not, take some time to confess and repent. Then receive God's forgiveness.

Exercise 3: Each One Reach One

God never delivers us from sin for our sakes alone. He expects us to use the experience first as a testimony to His power, faithfulness, and lovingkindness, and secondly, as a tool to help others. Think about a time that God delivered you from a sinful situation.

1. Write about your behavior and God's responses. Remember His mercy as well as any consequences you suffered as a result of the sin.

_____

_____

_____

_____

_____

2. Now, imagine talking to someone who is faced with falling into the same sin, under the same conditions. What would you tell him or her to possibly prevent that person from the same situation?

_____

_____

_____

_____

_____

3. What if you were faced with someone who has already fallen? What can you tell that person about the effects of sin, the feelings associated with that sin, and the pitfalls of it?

_____

_____

_____

_____

_____

4. Now, give that person hope. Talk to him or her about the power of God to deliver from sin, the hope to be found in a right relationship with God, and an opportunity to be cleansed from the stain and guilt of that sin because of Jesus Christ.

_____

_____

_____

_____

_____

Exercise 4: Undercover Sin

Jeremiah says our hearts are deceitful and wicked. Without the Spirit of God working in us, our hearts would lie to us all the time. As it is, one of the jobs of the Holy Spirit is to expose and exterminate the wickedness that lives within us. This is no small task because the holiness of God will not tolerate the smallest bit of deception. God sees the sin that is invisible to us. But if we allow Him to shine the truth of His Word on it, and we walk in that truth, our hearts become progressively purer.

There are many behaviors that fall into the category of sin, but because our hearts tell us that we "didn't really hurt anybody" or "we didn't really mean it," we don't see them as sins to confess and repent of. How many of the following situations apply to you?

1. Have you ever lied to someone to get off the phone?
2. Have you ever said something that was later found untrue, but never owned up to helping to spread the falsehood?
3. Have you ever said, "I love him, but I don't have to like him"?

4. Have you ever confessed to someone, but you weren't specific because you didn't think it was really any of his or her business?

5. Have you ever apologized to someone by shrugging and saying, "You know I didn't mean it," or "That's just the way I am"?

6. Have you ever spread gossip, thinking it was okay, because what you were telling was true?

7. Have you ever made fun of someone you didn't know and thought it was all right because he or she didn't know you or would never find out?

8. Have you ever been undercharged for something and called it a blessing, instead of correcting the oversight?

9. Ask God to show you the "little foxes" that eat away at your walk with Him.

Chapter 7
The Counterfeit of Godliness

> ... having a form of godliness but denying its power.
> And from such people turn away! For of this sort are
> those who creep into households and make captives of
> gullible women loaded down with sins, led away by
> various lusts, always learning and never able to come
> to the knowledge of the truth. Now as Jannes and
> Jambres resisted Moses, so do these also resist the
> truth: men of corrupt minds, disapproved concerning
> the faith; but they will progress no further, for their
> folly will be manifest to all, as theirs also was.
>
> 2 Timothy 3:5–7

At this juncture it is very important that we understand how godliness ought to govern our relationships. There is a real sense in which godliness should and will dictate whom you hang out with. Godliness will determine whom you enter into covenant with. It will determine your fellowship. This is by no means an exhortation to remove yourself from the realities of life. Godliness is a commentary on whom you let into your life, whom you trust, and whom you allow to influence your life.

Allowing yourself to be influenced by ungodly people means putting your own godliness in jeopardy. Paul was all too aware of the dangers of this. It was with the concern for counterfeit godliness that Paul challenged young Timothy and the church at Ephesus. He warned him of the dangers of living in the last days.

In 2 Timothy 3, Paul gave a portrait of the last days—that transitional span of time between the present times and the end times, beginning with the Lord's first coming and ending with His return. He did this because Timothy was pastoring the church at Ephesus and needed to be aware of the times and the signs of the times in which he lived. In fact, Paul began Chapter 3 by saying, "But know this, that in the last days perilous times will come." This was a warning to the young, struggling Timothy. He needed to be watchful, for these were dangerous times. He drew Timothy a spiritual map complete with landmarks, signposts, and pitfalls. He said there were specific things that would characterize the culture in the last days.

This was no doubt helpful to Timothy, who was trying to live out the call on his life. He tried to live holy in the last days. He tried to lead others to Christ. If you consider that the last days span the first and second coming of Jesus, you certainly realize that, like Timothy and Paul, we also are living in the last days. We also are pursuing godliness in the last days.

Now, Paul said if we look around, we will see certain events, people, activities, and behaviors that will mark these as the last days. As we go through the list, you might want to let your mind wander around your society, your neighborhood, your church, your family, even your own heart to see if you recognize these to be the last days.

Paul said in verse 2 that if we look around, we'll see people who "will be lovers of themselves, lovers of money, boasters, proud, blasphemers, disobedient to parents, unthankful, unholy, unloving, unforgiving, slanderers, without self-control, brutal, despisers of good, traitors, headstrong, haughty, lovers of pleasure rather than lovers of God." If you can look around and see anybody like that, it's a good indication that these are the last days. Violence, abortion, homosexuality, pornography, perjury, racism, hate crimes, juvenile delinquency, divorce, murder, police brutality, child abuse, domestic violence, shock media, and adultery mark these times. One look at the front page of any newspaper in any city in any country will tell you we're in the last days. If you were to tell the truth, you really don't have to look that far. Some of us don't have to look past the mirror.

But why were these times specifically highlighted? There was violence, persecution, and evil before the last days. There were unthankful, unholy men before this point in history. Old Testament Scripture is replete with examples of heady, high-minded, boastful, covetous pleasure-seeking men who loved many things more than they loved God. What separates these last days from every other time in history? Sin was nothing new in Paul's day. Wickedness was then, as it is now, a fact of life. Why then are these times so dangerous that Paul must warn Timothy—and us—about them?

It was not the tendency of the culture that concerned Paul. It was the target. Ungodliness in the last days has changed its focus. It has decided that the world is no longer adequate to satisfy it—it wants the Church. We know this because in Paul's exhortation he said the ungodly, unrighteous, unholy people of the last days will come "having a form of godliness." They will look like the Church. As long as the world looked like the world and the Church looked like the Church, we were okay. But Paul said in the last days, look out, because the world is putting on their Sunday best and raising hands and singing praises in an effort to infiltrate the house of God.

The Face of Phony Godliness

Before we examine the dangers of a world with an outward appearance of godliness, we should note that this means godliness has "a look." For those of you who are saved, sanctified, and filled with the precious Holy Ghost, you ought to know that there is an outward change that should have taken place subsequent to your salvation experience. Folks will either look at your life and know that you are God's child, or they'll look at your life and know that you are not.

They look godly on the outside. Paul said it will be difficult to spot the holy imposters because they will be clothed in the external expression of godliness. They will appear to be godly. They'll look just like Sister So-and-So who serves communion every first Sunday. They'll look just like Brother Whoever from the elder board or Sister What's-Her-Name who does a hallelujah dance every time the choir sings. All these people look godly on the outside. The Greek word for *form* here is *morphosis,* which means "a form or outward shape of." The emphasis is on the outside. In other words, if you observe them, everything you see will appear godly. But that is assuming you are observing only with your physical eyes and not with your spiritual ones.

They don't have the power of godliness. Paul said in verse 5 that the spiritual frauds will look godly, but you'll spot them as phony if you look for something that human eyes cannot see. He said they will have the form of godliness but "denying its power." In other words, they look godly, but their lives deny the very power that characterizes true godliness.

Let's work on that for a minute. True godliness presupposes power. What is the power that is supposed to be evident in a godly life? Ephesians 1:20–22 says it's the same power that raised Jesus from the dead, sat Him down at His Father's right hand, and dealt the devil his defeat. It is the power of God that moves in us and makes us capable to do all that He requires us to do. God's power gives us legs when we need to stand. It gives us peace in a storm and joy in temptation. God's power loves our enemies because we can't. It controls our tongues. It protects the weak and helpless when we'd rather protect ourselves. It is the power to bear the fruit of gentleness, humility, longsuffering, temperance and faith. It is the power to change us and change others through us. And it is the main thing that separates true godliness from its counterfeit.

This spiritual powerlessness has its behavioral manifestations. Paul illustrated, by example, the very essence of it. In 2 Timothy 3:8, Paul mentioned a couple of guys named Jannes and Jambres. They were two of the men who were in the court of Pharaoh when Moses went before him and told him to free the children of Israel. The Bible says Moses had a rod that the Lord told him to cast down. When Moses did as the Lord had commanded, the rod turned into a snake. That was the power of God. When Pharaoh saw this, he called two of his sorcerers or magicians. These were our boys Jan and Jam. Legend says these two brothers came with their own staffs mirroring the actions of Moses. They cast down their rods, and they, too, turned into snakes. That's just like the devil to try to beat God at His own game. Of course, the end of the story is that Moses' snake ate up the other two snakes, just as phony godliness dies in the face of a display of divine power of true godliness (Ex. 7: 11–22).

They resist the truth. Jannes and Jambres illustrate a giveaway characteristic of a godly pretender: They resisted the truth. They knew the truth. They looked at what Moses did, and they knew Moses was sent by God. They also knew that the source of their power was not God; yet they carried on as though they were as anointed as Moses. By confronting Moses with that display of cheap magic, Paul said they were resisting the truth, which means "to stand against it or in opposition to it." It's almost paradoxical when you think about it. When you resist the truth, you live a lie. But a lie, in order to be effective, must deceive someone, which means it must look like the truth. The actions of Jannes and Jambres looked like the truth to Pharaoh and the people watching. Beware of outward expressions of the truth that are untried by what God has already proven to be true—His Word and His power. A lie cannot stand in the face of truth anymore than darkness can stand in the face of light.

They have corrupt minds. The word *corrupt* means "to be spoiled or rotten." It is the picture of what happens when meat spoils. Paul said the minds of the ungodly are corrupt and rotten. The mind is the vein or channel to the heart. Salvation comes through the reasoning of the mind. That's why Scripture says, "Do not be conformed to this world, but be transformed by the renewing of your mind" (Rom. 12:2). It is the mind that is the door to the heart. When your mind is corrupt or rotten, it fills up your heart with the same corrupt, rotten stuff. Your mind feeds your heart rottenness; then your heart pumps rottenness into your lifestyle. When the truth enters your corrupt mind, your mind corrupts it and causes it to reach the heart as a lie. Your mind may be receiving the truth, day after day, Sunday in and Sunday out, but your life doesn't change. In order for the truth to change you, it has to go from your mind to your heart. It is with the heart that men believe unto salvation.

They can be proved to be phony. Lastly, they are "reprobate concerning the faith." *Reprobate* means "to test or investigate something, and when you have tested or investigated it, it comes up phony." It is the image of what happened in those days when gold was tested for impurities. In other words, it's like testing a gold coin and finding out it's only gold-plated. There are those who will come into your life who have only gold-plated godliness. They look godly and act godly. They pray, prophesy, teach, sing, preach, give, speak in tongues, dress, and smile with the godliness of angels. But when you test their lives against the standard of Jesus, they come up short. Gold is found impure only when it's tried. How many godly walks have you seen fold under the slightest discomfort of trial or the pressure of temptation? I'm not talking about those who strive with sin according to the will and power of the Holy Spirit. I'm talking about that brother or sister who says, "I'm sorry. I'll go to church every week, but I can't get with that celibacy thing!" Or the one who insists on living one way on Sunday and another way the other six days of the week. When their lives are tried in the furnace of the constraint of the Holy Spirit, they do not struggle. They turn back, proving all that glitters is not gold.

The Goal of Phony Godliness

The lives of godly phonies are masterpieces of external religion. They know the right way to do all the right things, to make the right impression on the right people. They know all the holy clichés: "Praise the Lord," "Hallelujah," "Thank You, Jesus," and "I'm blessed today, I'm blessed, blessed, blessed!" The key, though, is not in their mastery of Christian conduct. It's in the motive behind their mastery.

The Methods

Phony godly people have a strategy. They have a goal, which Paul pointed out in 2 Timothy 3:6. These are the kinds of people "who creep into households and make captives of gullible women." The Bible says these people prey on "gullible women," a phrase from a Greek word that means a "little woman" or "womanly woman." The suffix is diminutive, meaning a smaller or lesser or weaker version of woman, which was a put-down. Paul wrote this letter back in the first century in a patriarchal culture in which women weren't exactly walking equitably with men. So the language of that time contained a term that, though translated "gullible women," referred to anyone, male or female, who was weak-minded and weak-willed. It's not surprising, then, that such weak-minded and weak-willed people become easy targets for spiritual phonies who have methods that match their targets.

Creep into households. The first thing the phony does is creep into the houses or lives of their victims. The word creep means "to gain entrance by deception." This is not a person who sneaks into your life without you knowing it. It's not the person who just shows up one day when you're not watching. No, this person gets into your house, your home, your heart, and your life through the front door. Under ordinary circumstances, you would know not to let him in, but this time, he deceived you. He said the secret password. He pushed the right button, smiled the right smile. He was allowed to enter because he had a form of godliness. One version of this verse says he "worms his way" inside. These people are deceptively clothed in godly behavior wrapped up in pseudo righteousness. She's that sister who looks so godly to that brother. He's the man of God that woman of God has been praying for. These frauds feed on weak-willed, weak-minded saints. The weak ones are attractive to them and attracted to them. Their method is to creep. Their motive is to control. They come to control you, your life, and your destiny by capturing your weak mind.

Make captives. This phrase means "to take prisoner, as in a prisoner of war." These people deceive their way into a person's life, a life that was marked by spiritual weak-mindedness. Then they capture the mind of that person. If they can control the mind, then they have access to everything. If a man captures a woman's mind, she'll give him her body. If a woman captures a man's mind, he'll give her his money. That's why you've got to be careful about who or what controls your children's minds.

The godly fraud can so captivate you that you'll find yourself under the influence of pseudo religion and phony piety, doing things you know you shouldn't be doing, but can't help doing. You'll find yourself following one who seemed so holy and who seemed to be the answer to your godly prayers. Your life, mind, and heart will be taken prisoner. You're susceptible and vulnerable, because by capturing the mind, the fraud has captured the vehicle by which you are transformed and conformed to the image of Christ. Whoever has control of your mind, controls your destiny. The mind controlled by anything other than the Holy Spirit can only be bound for destruction.

That's why it is so important to remember Paul's exhortation in 2 Corinthians 10:5 to take captive every thought and make it obedient to Christ.

The Targets

Earlier we touched on the main target of the ungodly—those who are weak-minded. But weak-minded does not mean dumb. It has to do with a person being unable to overcome the appeal of pseudo-spiritual temptation. In the last days there will be people who have been assigned to your life by the enemy, who come into your life clothed as godly people. Their own lives are impotent because they don't possess the power that accompanies a truly godly walk. But Paul still warned us about them because they can be dangerous influences. So you have to ask yourself what attracts them to you? What could make you susceptible to them? What qualifies you as a target for those who play these dangerous spiritual games? Paul shows us in verses 6 and 7.

Loaded down with sins. How did the weak-minded get to be

that way? The text says they were loaded down, or laden, with sins. Laden is "the idea of continuing to add a load, to heap or pile on." To be laden with sins is to be weighted down with the burden of them. It is the accumulation of unconfessed sin. David said in Psalm 32 that his unconfessed sin was "heavy" upon him and soon it "turned [his] vitality into the drought of summer." One version says it "drained his sap." Allowing sin to accumulate without repentance makes a person weak.

Think of your heart as a plot of ground. The cleansing rain of forgiveness, which comes through confession and repentance, keeps it moist and receptive to the seeds of God's truth, which bring forth fruit unto godliness. Where there is no repentance, there is no rain. The soil becomes hard. The seeds fall on stony ground, and the truth does not take root. It is carried away with the first wind. Soon, even water won't penetrate.

A person laden with sin is one who is living a life of oppression by sin. The person carries it around all day, every day. Sin is not our load to carry. It was Christ's. We're not strong enough to carry the weight of our sin. We don't have the spiritual brawn to stand up under the heaviness of it. Sin quickly takes its toll on us and makes us weak. When we're weak, we're vulnerable. It's interesting that the Bible says spiritual phonies have a form of godliness, but their lives deny the very power of godliness. In reality, they're weak. Under normal circumstances—ones where we're not weighted down with our sin—we'd not only be able to recognize the ungodly, but we'd be able to withstand them. This is because they are weak, and we are strong enough to do all things through Jesus.

Sin paralyzes you. It keeps you from glorifying God, the purpose for which you were made. So you stay where you are, too weak to rise above your circumstances and too weak to operate effectively in them. If you've ever watched a nature show on television, you've no doubt seen that when carnivores prey on a group of animals, they always go after the smallest, weakest ones. They never set their sights on the strongest, healthiest ones. That's because the strongest animals can do two things: they can run fast, and if they can't run, they can fight hard. The odds tip dramatically in favor of the hunter when the prey is weak, slow, or handicapped in some way.

Every unconfessed sin is a weight hanging from you as you run the race to eternity. Each one slows you down, hinders you and fatigues you, making you awkward and clumsy. Scripture says you don't have to be fast or strong, but you do have to endure to the end. The heavier your load, the higher is your potential for collapsing before you reach the finish line.

Led away by various lusts. The word *lust* means "craving, passion, or desire." It includes, but is not limited to, sexual lust. To be led away by your lust means "to be swayed, pulled, or influenced by it." People who are targets for spiritual deception are those whose behavior is most often determined by the urging and prompting of their flesh. Deceivers are able to creep into their lives because they come carrying whatever the target craves, or needs, or has been praying for. Lust is neediness for something that will not glorify God, but will satisfy self.

James 4:3 says we ask and do not receive because we "ask amiss." In other words, we want to use what we've asked for to satisfy our own lusts rather than to glorify God. Some people pray for spouses, and they're not even equipped to be godly dates. They just want to have somebody. Some are praying for a raise in salary so they can buy a house, yet they don't give a dime of what they make now to the house of God. Satisfying lust breaks God's first commandment: You shall worship no other gods. Understand this: God is not going to give you anything that you will worship more than Him. So if temptation comes your way, He didn't send it. If it leads you away, you can be sure He's not the one shepherding you in that direction.

Satan makes sure that the ones he sends to worm their way into your life fit your taste buds. That way, if by some miracle you can see past their phony godliness, your flesh or lust won't let you get past their suitability to satisfy your craving *du jour*. The whole ploy of deception revolves around what is attractive or appealing to you. Your lust is defined by what appeals to you, and that's not limited to sexual things. You could have a lust for attention, a craving for flattery, or a desire for importance. You could need someone to tell you you're beautiful or smart or funny or spiritual or godly or anointed.

Whatever your need—importance, intimacy, affection, flattery, control—it is just another way to label what God calls lust. Any need that does not ultimately satisfy, glorify, or magnify the worthiness of God will lead you away from Him.

Always learning and never able to come to the knowledge of the truth. Second Timothy 3:7 says the weak-minded person is "always learning." So not only is this person laden with sin and driven by lust, he is also always taking in information. That's why I said earlier that the designation "weak-minded" does not imply stupidity. This is a person hungry for knowledge. This is a person who's always studying. This person attends your seminar, workshop, or convention. This person gets in anybody's healing line. He or she has the schedule of every evangelist coming to town.

I heard a story about something that happened at a seminar led by Reverend Charles Swindoll. A young man on the front row raised his hand and said, "Dr. Swindoll, Dr. Swindoll, do you remember me? I saw you the month before last at Trinity Seminary in Illinois. And I saw you when you spoke in Dallas!"

Dr. Swindoll replied, "When do you get to *practice* some of this stuff?"

Accumulating facts and information just for the sake of having them is a very subtle form of carnality. Your lust to learn for learning's sake is just that, lust, because it is motivated by selfishness and neediness and can often point to a craving to appear intelligent or godly to others. Your lustful craving to learn will make you less discriminating about who teaches you. Your desire to be seen as one who is biblically or spiritually literate, knows the Word, and knows the things of God can make you become careless about who teaches you. In your sometimes very sincere desire for more learning, you become susceptible to phony godliness.

There's a reason you become attractive to frauds who target you. Scripture teaches that though you are always learning, you are never able to come to the knowledge of the truth. The revelation of knowledge always requires a response to the revelation. This suggests that a person has a thirst to learn, learn, learn, but he never incorporates what he's learned into his lifestyle. It's the person who has reams of notes—sermon notes, class notes, and lesson notes dating from 1906. Now there's nothing wrong with the information, per se. The problem is that the information is still on the page. You keep learning the same stuff over and over. You're getting a lot of knowledge, but you're still at the spiritual equivalent of playing in the sandbox—you're intellectually fat but spiritually starving.

Notice the Scripture says "never able to come to the knowledge of the truth" (2 Tim. 3:7). Knowledge of the truth is the goal here. For the weak-minded person, it is the failing mark, the missed target. Knowledge is not the problem. Application is the problem. Godliness always assumes the application of accumulated knowledge. It always requires a response. Progressive revelation—that is, learning more as God is teaching you more—is always determined by progressive obedience. God will not give you high school revelation if you're still living a kindergarten life. We want a whale-sized anointing to fit our minnow-sized ministry. But God only shows us the next step after we've taken the first one. What does this mean to the person who is always learning? It means that much of the information he or she is collecting is useless. Why? Because the Holy Spirit leads us into all truth, and if we are being led by a need to learn, we'll never find the truth. If what we know doesn't get us to the truth, it's useless.

There is a saying that goes, "What you don't know can't hurt you." If you don't know the truth, trust me, it will hurt you. These "gullible women" never come to a knowledge of truth, which means they are as spiritually bankrupt as the phonies who prey on them. The Bible says "you shall know the truth, and the truth shall make you free" (John 8:32). Knowing the truth requires the Holy Spirit. If there is no truth, there is no Holy Spirit. If the Holy Spirit is not working, there is no power. If there's no power, you are as powerless as the powerless people who are preying upon you.

Not only can you not find the truth, you can't recognize the truth if you did find it. Discernment is the ability to know whether something is or isn't the Spirit of God. Simply put, it is the ability to see the truth. The phony has entered your life through deception. The only antidote for deception is discernment. Deception is an attempt to have you believe something is what it isn't. Discernment enables you to know something as it really is. Sin dulls our discernment because we are hardened in our heart and therefore not receptive to the truth. You become susceptible to phony godliness because you are operating in phony godliness.

The End of Phony Godliness

There are two exhortations in this 2 Timothy passage. These exhortations will apply to many of you who are reading this. But many of you to whom it applies will not obey.

I know that as some of you have been reading this chapter, God has convicted you. For some, you feel a little itching, nagging suspicion that has been confirmed by the revelation of the Spirit of God. You now realize you've been tricked and deceived. Others of you are not victims. You're the phonies. You're the ones playing the game. You're the deceivers. You're the ones who've been playing with and controlling someone's mind.

The first exhortation is to the saints who may already be or may become targets of phony godliness. It's found in verse 5. Two words: Turn away. Translation: Let it go. And when you let it go, you proceed in the other direction. You remember how Paul described the phonies as ones who resist the truth, have corrupt minds, and are reprobate concerning the faith? This means that the person who is controlling your life—who is in fact an ungodly person in a godly disguise, with ungodly motives—is not going to change. The reason many of you allow this person to remain in your life is because you're still waiting for the day when he or she is going to change. But the text says he's not going to change and she's not going to change.

The idea of resisting means "to deliberately stand in opposition to." We just talked about how both the victim and the perpetrator of phony godliness do not have the truth. The difference is that the weak-minded person, the "gullible woman," is looking for it. The phony is not only not looking for the truth, he has set himself firmly against it. He has made a decision, planted himself in a position, and committed himself to that position, which is opposed to the truth of God. Let him go. He is not going to change, and he will taint your walk of godliness and control your mind. God says, "Turn away."

Those nagging suspicions and questions are correct and coming to you by means of the Spirit. You hear God speak to your spirit right now. In His mercy He has moved past your spiritual blindness and cut through the hardness of your heart. Now you're seeing, perhaps, more clearly than you ever have. He says, "Turn away." Now listen to what God did not say. He did not say, "I'll take him away." He said, "[You] turn away." You must participate in your own deliverance. God will open the door, but you've got to be bold enough to walk through it in Jesus' name.

The second exhortation is to the spiritual imposters. Second Timothy 3:9 says that your folly shall be made manifest before all men. Translation: Your time is running out. God says he's about to turn the lights on to your game playing. Your deception is only for a season, then you will be exposed. The Word says you'll "progress no further." You'll be stopped in your tracks one way or another.

But there is hope. That game you're playing doesn't have to be a game. The very power you deny can still be accepted. Now, in order to live a life that is changed into a life of godliness, by the power of the Spirit of God, you have to submit. Stop trying to control other weak minds, and submit your mind to the transforming and renewing power of Jesus Christ. God will not force you to be godly. He will not make you stop being phony. As long as you're operating in a posture of deception, you will never change. The best thing you can do for that phony person is to let him go, because until you do, he'll never see a need to change.

Sometimes letting go helps shine the very light he needs to

see his corrupt life. Most people seem to seek a relationship with God that accommodates the status quo in their lives. This kind of spiritual schizophrenia leads a person in the futile venture of building a relationship with God while holding onto a relationship with ungodliness at the same time. They don't want to change and shun any principle that requires change. The result is a frail, fragile, phony godliness.

It's tough when God drops a word on us like this. It's much more comfortable to jump and shout and feel good. But godliness is practical. Godliness is real conduct in the real world. You cannot be godly and disregard God's Word. You cannot be the person God wants you to be if you're allowing others to control your walk with God. You cannot be the woman God wants you to be if you're manipulating and deceiving others.

These are the last days. Perilous times are upon us. The writer of Hebrews said we should "lay aside every weight, and the sin which so easily ensnares us, and let us run with endurance the race that is set before us" (Heb. 12:1). We cannot do that without resurrection power. That is the power of godliness.

Prayer
for
Discernment

Merciful Father, You have called us Your sheep
    and so we are.
We are helpless, armed with little more than
    our ability to cry out to You.
Without You we are weak, so we are often
    prey for those who seek to lead us away
    from You.
Please continue to show us our sin, that we
    might always be humble of spirit and
    contrite of heart.
Please protect us with Your Spirit of
    discernment and boldness so we will turn
    from anything or anybody that does not
    please You.
Let truth be the light that guides us through
    this world.
Let Your power, the power that raised our
    Savior, be the very breath by which we
    live.
And let us not seek to satisfy ourselves, but do
    all things, both great and small, to Your
    glory.
In Jesus' name, Amen.

Chapter 7 Exercises

Exercise 1: A Form of Godliness

  1. Memorize 2 Timothy 3:5–7:

". . . having a form of godliness but denying its power. And from such people turn away! For of this sort are those who creep into households and make captives of gullible women loaded down with sins, led away by various lusts, always learning and never able to come to the knowledge of the truth."

  2. Remember the characteristics of godly phonies:

- They appear godly
- They are powerless
- They resist the truth
- They have corrupt minds
- They are reprobate concerning the faith

  3. Remember the characteristics of a godly "target":

- They are loaded down with sins: Allowing sin to accumulate makes you weak under the load.
- They are led away by various lusts: The weak cannot resist the pull of the flesh.
- They are always learning and never able to come to a knowledge of the truth: Following the flesh can only lead you down a path away from Jesus, who is the Truth.

Exercise 2: The Power of Power, Part 1

Can you pinpoint times in your life when you knew you were without God's power? Think back to before you were walking with the Lord, or to a time that you may have fallen into sin.

1. What were the circumstances?
2. How did you feel?
3. How did your lack of power manifest itself in your behavior?
4. How did you get back on track?
5. Are there areas in your life where you still feel powerless or weaker than you'd like to be?
6. Take a moment to pray and ask God to show you why you feel this way.

Exercise 3: The Power of Power, Part 2

Now, think of times when you knew God's power was obviously working in you, for you, or through you. How did you know? Did the experience become a testimony to help someone else? What specifically did the incident teach you about God? List three situations.

Situation 1

_____

_____

_____

_____

Situation 2

_____

_____

_____

_____

Situation 3

_____

_____

_____

_____

Exercise 4: The Company You Keep

Read 2 Timothy 3:1–9 and answer the following questions:

1. What does this passage teach you about the importance of the people you associate with?

_____

_____

_____

_____

2. Are you "good company"? Why or why not?

_____

_____

_____

_____

3. Have you ever been "bad company"?

_____

_____

_____

_____

4. What do people learn about God when they keep company with you?

_____

_____

_____

5. What does this passage tell you to do about "bad company"?

_____

_____

_____

_____

6. What does this passage say God will do about "bad company"?

_____

_____

_____

_____

Part
Three
The Practice

Chapter 8
Training for Godliness

If you instruct the brethren in these things, you will be a good minister of Jesus Christ, nourished in the words of faith and of the good doctrine which you have carefully followed. But reject profane and old wives' fables, and exercise yourself toward godliness. For bodily exercise profits a little, but godliness is profitable for all things, having promise of the life that now is and of that which is to come.

1 Timothy 4:6–8

O ne weekend I was watching the sports news and heard something I had never heard before. A sportscaster was covering a Las Vegas boxing match. He reported that the match was stopped because one of the fighters had quit fighting in the middle of a round and started crying. This burly brother just broke down in the middle of the fight. They later learned that the fighter was physically, mentally, and emotionally unprepared to fight. The promoter said he had tried several times to convince the fighter's coach and trainers to cancel the bout because of concerns that the fighter had not completely recovered from a recent struggle with drug abuse. He told them that the man wasn't in any shape to box, but his camp insisted the fight go on as planned. So they put him in the ring, and shortly thereafter, this out-of-shape athlete gave what he had. When that ran out, he quit. And he cried.

Obviously he lost the fight. If he had won, it would have been a significant step in his career, putting him on track toward the championship. If his trainers had postponed the match, he might have won. But they didn't, and he lost. He lost because he was out of shape.

Many of you are losing the fight. You are losing spiritual battle after spiritual battle, not because you don't know Jesus, or because you doubt the promises of God, but because you're not spiritually fit.

In 1 Timothy, Paul painted a picture of an athlete who trained his body for competition. He counseled Timothy, his rookie minister, to train and prepare himself for spiritual competition. Paul said to be an effective minister, a true servant of the Lord, Timothy needed to exercise himself on a spiritual level. Paul said, by comparison, that bodily or physical exercise is good, but its benefits are limited to the body, which is purposed to serve us only temporarily, only in this life.

But spiritual fitness, or godliness, has lasting value. Its benefits carry the believer through this life and the life to come. As believers we should prepare ourselves spiritually for the challenges and battles of our Christian walk. Paul urged us to get in shape and stay in shape.

The Option of Training

The first thing we must realize is that, although we may be saved, training is not a requirement; it's an option. In 1 Timothy 4:6, Paul used an interesting phrase to advise Timothy on how to minister to the people of God. He said if Timothy put the brethren "in remembrance of these things," he would be a good minister. Paul was a veteran spiritual leader, speaking to a spiritual son. He basically told Timothy that as a leader and pastor of God's people at Ephesus, there were several things he must do.

First, he was to keep the brethren in remembrance of godly behavior. Paul did not tell Timothy to order God's people to be godly, but instead to bring the things they needed for godliness to their remembrance. The phrase *put in remembrance* means "to lay or spread before someone." It does not suggest a forceful command, but an exhortation, counsel, or advice. It lies somewhere between a warning and a suggestion. Paul wanted Timothy to keep his flock reminded of what they were already supposed to be, to keep their goal before them, and to encourage them in their walk with Christ. If the focus and spotlight could be kept on what they knew about God, they would be motivated to godliness. Timothy was charged to persuade, rather than command.

Choosing Godliness

Believers are not commanded to be godly. But we are exhorted or encouraged to godliness as a part of God's perfect design. God has graciously given believers free will. He wants us to voluntarily choose to reflect and model His character. We are holy because we are His. Because we are His, we should want to be like Him, which is godly. Holiness puts us in a position to be godly.

Return to our thumbnail definition of godliness: consistent conduct that is consistent with the character of God. It all begins with knowing the nature and character of God, which is an ongoing and dynamic process for believers. It requires a lifetime commitment, and the benefits are many. God is the revelation of truth, which tells me that the more I know Him, the more I will love Him. As I love Him more, I want to serve Him more. Serving Him makes me want to please Him. The more I want to please Him, the more I want to bring glory to Him. And the more glory I bring to Him, the godlier I become.

Glorifying God Is Both the Goal and the Reward of Godliness

I can't please God by saying I'm His child. God puts the ball in my court. Godliness is walking; it is putting feet to my faith. Godliness challenges me to live a life that, through my actions, consistently demonstrates I am God's child. When you know you are God's child and act like it—that's godliness.

So if holiness relates to position and godliness relates to practice, then it is possible to be holy and ungodly. Consider why you are holy. You are holy because God made you holy when he separated you unto Himself. After He granted us holiness, He asked us to behave as though we are holy—that's godliness.

Godliness is defined by our conduct. The two have to go together. Maybe this example will help illustrate my point. Positionally, you are your mother's child. You were born to her and no other mother. But you can be hers positionally and not act like it. Some of the worst whippings I ever got were not because I had ceased to be Ruth Ulmer's son, but because I was not acting like Ruth Ulmer's son. My parents had set a certain standard for me, a standard that was determined by who they were as my parents, not who I was as their child. I was disciplined when I fell below the standard they set. At times, I acted as if I belonged to them. Similarly, you can be God's son or daughter in position, yet, in your everyday walk, be as ungodly as someone who does not belong to Him.

I am not godly until I begin to act like it. Holiness is what you are. Godliness, however, is practical holiness. Believers are to be reminded that they are holy and should therefore flesh out that holiness through godliness. In other words, God wants us to consistently display conduct that tells the world who He is as our Father.

According to Paul, a pastor's responsibility is to keep his congregation in remembrance of godliness, to saturate them with the sanctity of the Savior to a degree that they see so much of Him, they can't help but love Him and serve Him. Ministers are not to command individuals to be godly. They are to teach who God is—expose God's character, so believers will then love Him who has revealed Himself. The love that believers have for Him will then be fleshed out in conduct. If you want to evaluate your success as a pastor, examine the lives of your flock. Are their lives changed by what God has revealed to them through you? Help them make the choice to go toward godliness.

Practical Training

It is no accident that Paul used an athletic metaphor to describe the pursuit of godliness. Paul knew there was the potential for victory or loss, so to assure our victory in this spiritual contest, he warned us to exercise. In 1 Timothy 4:7 he used the verb *train*, which is the Greek word *gumnazo*, which is where we get our word *gymnasium*. The word speaks of not just training, but of "the focused discipline behind the training." Discipline demands commitment and consistency. You will never become godly by accident—an attitude of discipline must precede the pursuit of godliness.

The attitude of one who would be godly, is first and foremost, one of focus. Satan has any number of distractions waiting in the wings to keep us off the track toward godliness. Some of them are even good things—but not better than becoming like God. The way to keep our focus is to, as the book of Hebrews encouraged us, "fix our eyes on Jesus" (12:2 NIV).

But simply having a goal and focus is not enough. Physical exercise requires sustained, rigorous effort. It is not easy. Spiritual exercise is no different. Displaying the character of Christ is work. It is the result of making a conscious decision to live your life based on who you are in Christ. Godliness is an act of volition. You must choose to walk, live, and act godly. It demands personal responsibility and commitment, which grow out of knowing who God is and knowing how committed He is to you. Once you understand that, then Paul said exercise.

But be aware that exercise is never done in the actual competition. It only prepares you for the competition. Once the contest starts, it's too late to get into shape. When the bell rings or the first gun goes off, it's too late to try and get in fifty crunches or a set of leg lifts. After the coin is tossed and positions are taken, this is not the time for skipping rope or jumping jacks. You have to be in shape before the game starts to have a chance at winning.

Spiritual exercise begins with Bible study, prayer, meditation, and fasting. It continues when we practice instant obedience to God's will. We expand that exercise by allowing God to reign in our lives. Spiritual exercise is to be woven into the very fabric and foundation of our lives. That requires commitment, discipline, perseverance, and longsuffering. We can only grow to be the people God wants us to be when we allow our exercise to secure our foundations and stretch our abilities.

Your Personal Trainer

I learned a secret. People who make the most dramatic advances in physical fitness have a personal trainer. Without someone guiding you, you just randomly work out. Most of us don't have the kind of discipline we need, so we hire personal trainers.

John 14:26 says: "But the Helper, the Holy Spirit, whom the Father will send in My name, He will teach you all things, and bring to your remembrance all things that I said to you." The Helper is a translation of the word *paraclete*. Paraclete means "to call alongside." The paraclete, which is the Holy Spirit, will stand alongside you as your personal trainer.

His Role

The Holy Spirit, as our trainer for godliness, has the perfect approach and methods designed to succeed.

He reminds you of what you know. Whenever you begin a training program, some of what the trainer tells you is nothing new. When the trainer tells you to eat certain things and not others, there is no great news flash in your spirit. You've heard it before. Stay away from ice cream. Close your mouth to pie. Pull away from the table when the cake comes around. It's nothing new, but the trainer reminds you of these things—things you've heard before, never acted on, or stopped acting on. This is also one of the roles of the Holy Spirit in spiritual fitness. He reminds you of all those useful things you have been learning all along.

He teaches you what you don't know. In John 16:13, Jesus said the Holy Spirit "will guide you into all truth; for He will not speak on His own authority, but whatever He hears He will speak; and He will tell you things to come." The word *guide* means "to show the way in unknown territory." God uses the Holy Spirit to grow and edify you, stretch and mature you, to build you up, then take you to the next level of spiritual maturity. It's a level that you have never seen before. It is unknown territory. But you are promised a personal trainer who is the Spirit of truth. He will come alongside you to guide you in the new place.

He knows what you need. There is a strange dynamic that occurs between a trainer and trainee. The trainee is always complaining to the trainer about what he can't do. The truth of the matter is that a good trainer knows more about the trainee than the trainee does. He knows where he's weak and where he's strong. He knows how quickly his muscles will respond to certain kinds of training. He knows when he's really tired or just being lazy. A really good trainer can look at you and tell you if you've been eating the right foods or if you've gotten enough sleep the night before. The trainer knows the trainee's past history. He puts the trainee on an exercise program tailored for his needs to achieve the desired goal. Always during exercise, the trainer is right there, next to the trainee. He never goes on a coffee break. He never turns his back.

He takes you to the next level. Whenever the trainer puts the trainee into weight-lifting position, the trainer makes sure there is enough weight on the bar to help the trainee advance to the next level. When the trainee gets in weight-lifting position, the trainer is right there, whispering into his ear, "You said you wanted to get stronger. You said you wanted to grow. You said you wanted to build endurance and stamina. Now, lift that weight." The Holy Spirit will encourage you by reminding you of the prize of God's high calling. He'll remind you of times past when you thought you couldn't carry the weight of your problems, but He was right there showing you how. Sometimes the trainee tries to negotiate with the trainer. He'll say his load is too heavy or that the trainer requires him to lift too much weight. "Would you please, sir, take off some of this weight?" But the trainer knows what his pupil needs. He tries to help the trainee get stronger. He knows the trainee only gets stronger by lifting something heavy. Likewise, the Holy Spirit knows you can't exercise yourself unto godliness by doing what you're used to doing, what's easy to do. He knows you have to go through pain sometimes. He knows you have to be taken to new plateaus of faith, new levels of understanding in the Word, greater depths in meditation, and further intimacy in prayer.

He stands ready to help. He will never turn his back on you, because He's also your spotter. If He sees you straining and sweating and about to throw in the towel, He takes notice. A good trainer always stands close enough to place one finger on the load you're trying to lift. If it looks like the bar is about to fall, a good trainer will hold it for a spell to give you some rest. He's there to make sure you don't collapse under too much weight. After all, He's got a promise to keep: "God is faithful, who will not allow you to be tempted beyond what you are able" (1 Cor. 10:13). He'll never let the bar fall on you and injure you.

Do you know what it's like to struggle with a heavy load only to have God step in to let you rest? God puts His Holy Ghost finger underneath your load and lifts it for you. In the midst of your struggle, you find yourself able to lift your burden. Before you know it, you hear something in your ear. Before you know it, you're getting stronger. You're able to lift up your problems, discouragement, and heartache. The power of the Holy Ghost helps you to run on in Jesus' name. If you keep working out with your Holy Ghost trainer, you'll find after awhile that your burden feels a little bit lighter. It's not really lighter; it's just you've gotten bigger spiritual muscles. You have the joy of the Lord, which is your strength. You've got heaven in your view.

He gets results. I go to the gym regularly. I've noticed that people who leave the gym have a walk about them. They have a little more glide in their stride. They may not even have lost any weight, but they know that as long as they keep going to the gym, one day the pounds will come off. If you're regularly exercising spiritually, you know your troubles will come off. You know your trials will one day be a thing of the past. You know discouragement won't be with you always. You might as well start thanking your Trainer right now, even if you haven't lost a pound. You know, if you're exercising spiritually, that He's the best Trainer there is. And if you look around at some of His other clients, you know that those who stick with Him see miraculous results.

Our Response

But as surefire as the Holy Spirit's program is, it will only succeed if we respond. Not only is He our Trainer, we are to live our life according to His direction.

In the fifth chapter of Paul's letter to the Galatians, Paul used phrases like "walk in the Spirit," "be led by the Spirit," and "live in the Spirit." Rather than go into a detailed exegesis of these passages, let me simply say that the operative word in each phrase is *Spirit*—the Holy Spirit of God. God's ideal for the believer is that we live our lives in the realm of the Holy Spirit. Walking in the Spirit—the exercise we should strive for—refers to one's lifestyle. In other words, we are to live lifestyles characterized by the Person and work of the Spirit of God. To be led by the Spirit suggests that same Spirit directs our lifestyle. It means we allow Him to point the way, to navigate us through the turns and intersections of life.

You might notice that the phrase "walk in the Spirit" appears in verse 15 and again in verse 25. The Greek word for the first instance of *walk* is *peripateo*, the normal word for walk as a physical action. However, the word used for the second instance for *walk* is less common. It is the word *stoicheo*. This word has several significant connotations. First of all it means "to walk in a straight line, to behave properly." The word was used for movement in a definite line, as in military formation or in dancing. Here it means "to walk in a straight line or to conduct one's self rightly." This is to be a continual and habitual action. Walking in the Spirit means "to line up my life behind the Holy Spirit and let Him lead me."[1]

When I was in the Marine Corps, one of the few things that

I liked about military service was close order drill. Talk about a personal trainer! I loved the melodic way the drill sergeant barked out the commands to us gawky, uncoordinated recruits. One of the most amazing transformations was to see military geeks being gradually molded into real Marines. One of the most dramatic indications that we were transitioning into real Marines was the surprise, one day, that we were marching in time, in line. Two reminders of what was needed to drill with excellence were the commands *cover* and *alignment*. These commands meant to make sure you were in line neatly behind the person in front of you and in line with the person beside you, respectively. The key to synchronized drill was to be in such a united relationship with the other Marines around you that you stepped together. We actually breathed together.

When the Bible says we are to walk in the Spirit, I have a picture in my mind of marching behind the Holy Spirit as my Divine Drill Sergeant. I must continually ask myself if I am keeping my cover and alignment. When I was in perfect alignment and perfect cover with the Marine in front of and beside me, if a person stood at the front of my column, I could not be seen. I was hidden behind the other Marines. Paul said if you are truly walking in the Spirit—in line with the Spirit, maintaining your cover and alignment—you can't be seen; only He can be seen. When people look at you, they see Him. When you speak, He speaks. Walking in the Spirit is not so much you becoming an extension of God the Holy Spirit, but the Spirit of God living in you, living through you, touching lives through you, and blessing others through you.

Walking in the Spirit means you stay in line with God. It means you don't break the line. It means you don't get out of line. You don't move until it is your turn. It means you live your life following the lead of the Holy Spirit.

Some of you are losing battles you should be winning because you're not in shape. It's not just that Satan and his imps are on your trail. Some demons can't be cancelled out. They have to be cast out. Jesus said some demons come out only by fasting and prayer. Fasting and prayer are essential exercises. Some of you are holy but ungodly. You come to church every Sunday, but you're not in shape. You can't work out once a week and expect to see results. Walking through the gym once a week does not get you in shape. God has called you to be a godly woman or a godly man. He wants your relationship with Him to be manifested in your conduct and actions. Godliness is not measured by your behavior in church or the way you conduct yourself in the spotlight. God wants you to leave your church seat, walk out of the door back out into the world, and do what He has called you to do, the way He has called you to do it.

Few pastors are calling people to godliness. Pastors are tailoring sermons to fit the exercise of their congregation, showing them how to access the riches of God, making the aim the blessing. The aim should be the One from whom all blessings flow. People of God are working to get stuff—more money, bigger houses, nicer cars. But effective ministry, ministry for the kingdom of God, can only flow out of a godly lifestyle. All gain beyond Christ is not true gain, but a weight that hinders our progress toward God.

It's time to get in shape. Sign up for a heavenly gym membership. There's open enrollment. And what a deal! The price was paid in full at Calvary. But don't be satisfied with just signing up. Go on and work out. Stick with the program. You'll soon see the results you've been looking for.

Prayer
for
Spiritual Fitness

Almighty God, You are my strength, my
      comfort, and my light in this dark world.
I know there will be times of trial and suffering
      in my life.
Your Word says so.
But I know that Your Word also says You will
      prepare me to face any trial with peace
      and joy.
Lord, show me how to make the most of my
      time in prayer with You.
Teach me how to quiet my spirit that I might
      meditate more effectively on You.
Reveal Yourself to me in Your Word, and show
      me how to consecrate myself to You
      through periods of fasting.
I don't want to miss an opportunity to serve
      You because I haven't prepared myself to
      walk worthy of You.
Lord, show me who You say I am.
Show me my weaknesses and exercise me until I
      am usable by You for Your glory.
Build me up.
Strengthen me.
Change me.
In Jesus' name, Amen.

Chapter 8 Exercises

Exercise 1: A Spiritual Workout

1. Memorize 1 Timothy 4:8: "Bodily exercise profits a little, but godliness is profitable for all things, having promise of the life that now is and of that which is to come."

2. Spiritual exercise involves study, prayer, meditation, fasting, worship, and immediate obedience to the commands of God. Are you working on these things in your life?

3. Our spiritual "personal trainer" is the Holy Spirit. He is the One who guides us in our walk with the Lord. Do you know where you are being led concerning all truth? Do you know where you're going concerning things to come?

4. Glorifying God is both the goal and the reward of godliness. Read 1 Corinthians 10:31 and Romans 8:18 for more insight into this truth.

Exercise 2: Out of Shape?

Think of a time when you gave up on something because you were not spiritually fit enough to stick with it.

1. How could you have been better able to handle the situation? Were you praying, fasting, studying, or meditating to discover God's place in it?

_____

_____

2. If the same task or opportunity presented itself to you tomorrow, could you see it through? Why or why not?

_____

_____

3. What are some Scriptures you know now that you didn't know then that could have helped guide you in the situation?

_____

_____

Exercise 3: Toning Up

Sometimes we need a little toning up to keep our muscles in shape between times of heavy lifting. Likewise, spiritual toning is a way to keep things from sagging between trials. Following are some toning Scriptures. Write them down and read them periodically. Try to commit as many of them to memory as you can.

Philippians 4:13	Philippians 1:6
Proverbs 8:17	Proverbs 3:5,6
Isaiah 26:3	Psalm 119:165
Psalm 103:12	1 Thessalonians 5:24
2 Corinthians 3:17	Jeremiah 29:11
John 14:18	Isaiah 43:1
1 Peter 5:6	1 John 4:11
Psalm 147:3	

Exercise 4: Growing You in God

1. Think about what you know to be true about God. How has it changed you, helped you, and nurtured you?

_____

_____

2. Now listen. Are there areas in your life where He would like to train you or take you to another level? Write about what comes to mind.

_____

_____

3. Pray with your heart. If you're not sure how to start, use the prayer path provided (Prayer for Spiritual Fitness, p. 179). Don't forget to thank Him.

Chapter 9

The Course of Godliness, Part 1:
From Revelation to Maturity

> *Those who trust in the LORD*
> *Are like Mount Zion,*
> *Which cannot be moved, but abides forever.*
> *As the mountains surround Jerusalem,*
> *So the LORD surrounds His people*
> *From this time forth and forever.*
>
> *For the scepter of wickedness shall not rest*
> *On the land allotted to the righteous,*
> *Lest the righteous reach out their hands to iniquity.*
>
> *Do good, O LORD, to those who are good,*
> *And to those who are upright in their hearts.*
>
> Psalm 125:1–4

*I*n most Bible translations, just under the title of Psalm 125 you will see a line or a subheading that says "A Song of Degrees" or "A Song of Ascents." Psalms 120 through 134 are all songs of degrees or ascents. These songs of ascents became the songs the tribes of Israel and their families would sing on their way up to Jerusalem three times a year for their national feast days.

You've probably heard songs like "We Are Marching Up to Zion" and "We Are Going Up to Jerusalem." As you read through this group of psalms, several of them give you the idea or feeling of going up. Psalm 121 says, "I will lift up my eyes." Psalm 122 says, "I was glad when they said to me, / Let us go into the house of the Lord." The city of Jerusalem is geographically on a hill. When you fly into Tel Aviv, you board a bus and then you begin to ascend. You must go up the hill. God has placed an entire city on top of this hill.

The psalmist sets the scene in Jerusalem, also called Zion, which was the location of the temple. Mount Zion is a multi-dimensional term that at one time might have meant the entire city of Jerusalem. At other times it described a particular hill or a specific mountain within the city. In this context, it really refers to the city in general, more specifically what is called the Temple Mount, also known as Mount Zion.

Aside from the geography of Jerusalem, this passage also speaks about something of the geography of godliness. The promises made in Psalm 125 that were sung by these worshipers on their way up to the temple applied only to a particular kind of person: "those who trust in the Lord are like Mount Zion." Their goal, their destination, was Mount Zion, which was symbolic of spiritual maturity or belief in action. They were set on a path straight for it, and they knew their destination. The same is true for all believers. The goal for our course, as theirs was, should be to move from spiritual infancy to maturity.

The Pilgrimage to Zion

Prior to coming to Jerusalem, the mountain or geographical location that had been most significant in the life and history of Israel was Mount Sinai. This is the mountain upon which God gave the revelation of His Word, His will, and His way. It is where the Torah—what we call the Pentateuch or the first five books of the Bible (Genesis, Exodus, Leviticus, Numbers, and Deuteronomy)—was delivered to the people of Israel through Moses. (In the Torah God gave them specific guidelines about how to worship Him and how to treat one another.) Mount Sinai symbolizes the revelation of God, given when Israel was a young infant nation after they were led out of bondage from Egypt. While on their way to Jerusalem, they stopped at Mount Sinai. Mount Sinai was never intended to be a destination or a goal, just a stop along the way where God revealed His Word. The children of Israel were never going to Sinai; they were always going through Sinai. They were never supposed to set up permanent residence there. God took them through Sinai to Jerusalem (Zion), the land overflowing with milk and honey.

The ascent from Sinai to Zion is symbolic of a spiritual journey of maturity, a pilgrimage from revelation to relationship. Sinai was where the people of God received God's Word, but that Word was to be fleshed out or expressed ultimately on Zion. If Sinai was the mountain of revelation, Zion was the mountain of relationship. God is not satisfied simply with your receiving a revelation of His will. The revelation of God is significant only if it translates to your relationship with God. You must become a doer of the Word, not just a hearer. Your spiritual growth will be stunted if you remain at Sinai. Going on to Zion, however, is the manifestation and expression of relationship.

Many of us want to camp out at the point of revelation. But to stop at revelation just short of relationship is to miss God's plan for your life. It was at Sinai that God told His people what to do. It was at Zion that they did it. At Sinai their belief in God was affirmed by the giving of His Word. At Zion that belief was turned into behavior, and that's what spiritual maturity is. Spiritual maturity is not just gaining intellectual facts. It's not just knowing more about God. It's knowing God. It's not just knowing what to do. It's doing what you know to do. Many of us are halted in our spiritual growth because we are satisfied and complacent at Sinai. If the truth were told, most of us are educated far beyond our obedience. In fact, if God didn't tell you anything else, you could probably spend the rest of your life trying to do what He's already told you to do.

We have to be careful that we don't become satisfied with just receiving God's Word, that we don't become satisfied just coming to church on Sunday. As a matter of fact, a lot of us are just plain fat with the Word. God's Word is food. Food is fuel, and fuel is the power that moves us. God's Word should be taken in and used as fuel for godliness. It should manifest itself in our daily lives. God's goal for us is not that we simply receive His Word, but that we incorporate it into our lives and move from Sinai to Zion, from revelation to relationship. That's called going and growing. God has called us to grow in Him. God has called us to maturity.

The People of Zion

Psalm 125 begins by saying that those who trust in God will be like Mount Zion. Becoming like Mount Zion is the promise. But the promise is one of limited reach. It has qualifications and restrictions attached to it. It only includes a particular type of individual. I would suggest to you that Psalm 125 is a psalm of promise for the godly, for those whose conduct is consistent with the character of God.

First of all, those who receive the promise contained in Psalm 125 are those who place their trust in the Lord. The word *trust* means "to attach oneself to." It is not the picture of someone who is afraid and therefore clinging. It is more accurately the image of someone who has a sense of confidence and boldness because of the One to whom he or she is attached. It implies that the one attached is not worried or afraid. In fact, the opposite is true. The one attached is almost carefree in his or her comfort. The attached has a sense of security because the One he or she relies on is One who brings hope and deliverance. Trusting God in this context means you are securely relying upon Him because you know He is secure. God says those who are trusting and relying upon Him shall be like Mount Zion.

The second characteristic of those who will become like Zion is that they will be good. Verse 4 says, "Do good, O LORD, to those who are good." Even Jesus said to a man who called Him good, "Why do you call me good? No one is good but One, that is, God." So when the psalmist talks about those who are good, he is simply referring to those who are like the Father, or those who are like God. To be like God is to be godly. Those who are good have lives that reflect the goodness and character of God, because no one is good except the Father. Goodness only comes out because of the God that resides in them.

The third characteristic is that they are upright in their hearts. An upright heart has to do with direction. It refers to those whose hearts are set on God. The focus of their lives is God. This godly person is not so much one who is perfect, but one whose goal is to be like God. Dr. Jack Hayford said this: "God is always more concerned about your direction than your perfection, for if we labor with imperfection, He can correct that . . . if we're going in the right direction."[1] God can handle your imperfections as long as you stay on the right road. To be a person with an upright heart is to be a person whose heart, whose goals, whose life, whose focus, is God. God says those whose heart is right before Him, whose direction is toward Him, are like Mount Zion.

The Place of Zion

What does it mean for the godly person to "be like Mount Zion"? If God can find a person who will attach himself to Him, reflect the goodness of Him, and has a heart focused on Him, he will be like Mount Zion. Psalm 125:1 says Mount Zion is a mountain that cannot be removed. The word *removed* means "it cannot be shaken loose or shaken out of place." One version says, "whose feet will not slip." Those who are godly will be like Mount Zion in the sense that they will not be removed from wherever God has established them. It's the same idea that's found in Psalm 121, also a psalm of degrees, which says: "He will not allow your foot to be moved." God will not allow you to stumble or slip if you keep your trust in Him, if your life continues to reflect His goodness, and if your heart is positioned toward Him.

The man or woman who lives a life of godliness is unmovable, like a mountain. Not like sand that shifts, not like the wind rustling, not like the waves crashing here and there, but as you walk in righteousness with God, you shall be as a mountain. The image here is one of stability and firmness, even when there is a sudden shaking or a sudden rumbling that seeks to move you from whatever you're attached to. The man or woman whose life is centered and focused and planted and relying upon God, will live a life that will be firm no matter what comes along to try to shake it loose.

God will make sure your foot won't slip. He will always make sure that when you step and stand, you will always be on solid ground. When you are attached to Him and relying on Him, He says you will be as unmovable as the mountain.

Psalm 125 goes on to describe the relationship of the mountain to the geography of the rest of the area. It says, "As the mountains surround Jerusalem, / So the LORD surrounds his people." Zion is set on a mountain. Surrounding it on three-quarters of its sides are more mountains. On the east side there is the Mount of Olives. Then there is the Mount of Ill Counsel, which is where the house of Caiaphas was. This is the place where Peter denied Christ three times. There is another hill or mountain called the Mount of Reproach. This is where Solomon worshipped idols. So there are mountains, mountains, and more mountains; and in the middle is Mount Zion. First God makes you a mountain, then He surrounds you with mountains. You are fixed and stable; then He surrounds you with more stability.

Now, to the northeast of Zion is a mountain called Mount Scopus. Mount Scopus looks down on Zion. The name means "the mountain of viewing." It is a mountain above the other mountains. Little or nothing can take place on Zion that cannot be seen from Mount Scopus. Get the picture? God makes you a mountain. Then He surrounds you with mountains. Everything that happens on your mountain can be seen from His mountain. You are Zion, and God is Scopus. Zion is where you serve God by worshipping Him. While you're serving, God is scoping. Whatever happens to you can be seen by God, who watches your life from a vantage point of complete illumination. Not only can He see everything, He sees it before you do. Remember He surrounds you, and He's higher than you.

God sees you. There are no news flashes or bulletins with Him. He does not need Dan Rather or Peter Jennings to tell Him what's going on. He doesn't need CNN. He doesn't need the morning paper, a cellular phone, or a satellite cable. You can lie down every night with the assurance that everything that happened to you today, God saw. Everything you will go through tomorrow, He already knows. He's already seen the movie. In fact, He directed the movie, so He already knows how it's going to end. In the end you win. He wrote the ending of this story before He laid the foundations of the world. He knew the outcome before He put the mountains in their places, before He put you in your place.

God sees you right where you are. You don't have to come from where you are to where He is in order to be seen. God sees what you are going through. He knows what you're feeling. He saw where you were going before you got where you were going, and He's already made provisions to bring you out of it. He has already provided a way of escape that you may come through it victoriously, praising God all the way. He has fixed it so that no matter what comes, you have everything you need to handle it. Now, if you can't handle it, He won't let it come. But if it does come, it didn't sneak past Him, because He is Mount Scopus.

Some of you thought God had forgotten about you. You thought He had lost your file or misplaced your address. You thought His computer had crashed. He has not forsaken you. I don't care what you're going through. I don't care what you're wrestling with. I don't care what you're struggling with. There is nothing that cannot be seen from where God sits. You may be on a hilltop, or you may be in a dungeon. You may be in sunshine or under the clouds. Wherever you are, God sees you right where you are. He neither sleeps nor slumbers. He never even blinks. He doesn't go on vacation or take a coffee break. His eye is always on you.

Psalm 61:2 says, "Lead me to the rock that is higher than I." The problem with some of you is that you're looking for God in low places. The psalm says, in essence, "Give me a rock that is higher than I am"—a rock that can take me up, move me out of my circumstances, not comfort me in them. Sometimes we need to change our altitude in order to change our attitude. Some of you are in the valley with some teeny tiny pebbles keeping you company. God is trying to take you up to the mountain, to a place of real security and safety. Now, in case you're wondering, He can see you in that valley too. But He loves you enough to want to set you up above some things.

Some people want to keep you down. The devil will try to trick you into thinking that God doesn't see you where you are. If that doesn't work, He'll tell you that God doesn't understand your pain. He can't relate to what you're going through, so He doesn't know how hard it is for you. A woman at our church had a son who died tragically. For a long time she said she was very angry with God. She was so angry and bitter. Finally, she gathered up all of her righteous indignation to go before God and complain to Him. In anger, she said to Him, "Where were you? How could you let this happen? How could you allow this? You saw my son. You knew he was in danger, and you let him die. You said you'd never leave me. Where were you when my son died?" She said God spoke to her heart immediately, "The same place I was when My Son died. I was on the throne."

God sees you in your struggle. He sees you in that trial. He sees that secret heartache. He sees that broken heart. He sees that private pain. He sees that thing you can't tell anyone about. He sees that confusion that no one else can fix. God takes notice of everything that happens in your life. He's concerned about everything that happens.

Let me ask you a few questions. Do you think that you can have a problem that God doesn't know about? God is omniscient, all-knowing. Do you think you have a problem that God doesn't care about? God knows and He cares. So then, do you think you have a problem in which God is powerless? Do you think you have a problem that God can't handle?

There is a site in Israel called the Garden Tomb, it is traditionally thought to be the spot where Jesus was buried. Just on the inside of this little tomb, there's a sign on the door that says, "He's not here. He has risen just as He has said." Now listen closely. Jesus Christ, the Son of the almighty God, died, and God raised Him from the dead. Here's what that means: If your problem is not bigger than a dead Savior, God can handle it.

The Protector of Zion

As the mountains surround Jerusalem, so God surrounds His people. There are mountains on the east, on the northeast, on the south, on the southwest, and on part of the west. But up in the northwest corner, overlooking Jerusalem, there is a gap. So you've got mountains, mountains, and more mountains, and then a gap where the mountains are much lower, more like foothills. So it makes sense that when a nation would attack Israel, they would attack from the north. As safe as Jerusalem was, on a mountain and surrounded by mountains, there was still that gap, that area of vulnerability where the city was exposed and susceptible to attack.

Likewise, the people of God are always vulnerable to the attack of the enemy. We are born with some areas of vulnerability, some are forced upon us, and still others we create. We are born with a natural bent toward sin and a natural desire toward fulfilling the lust of our flesh. Our environment can also provide areas of weakness. A girl who grows up in an abusive home becomes a woman more likely to accept abuse from a spouse. A boy who has been poor all his life becomes a man ruled by money—either he doesn't know how to hold on to it, or he holds on to it too tightly. Then there are the areas of vulnerability we create for ourselves through willful, deliberate sin. Sin weakens us and makes us ready prey for the enemy. So, in spite of the fact that you trust God, reflect the goodness of God, and are focused on Him, there are still gaps in the mountains that surround you. But remember, God sees everything, including the gaps.

Psalm 125:3 promises that "the scepter of wickedness shall not rest / On the land allotted to the righteous." In other words, the rod, which is the weapon of the enemy, will not rest on the righteous. Shall not rest means "shall not continue forever." Once the rod has been laid to God's people, it won't stay there.

As I've said before, there is no "battle elimination clause" in your salvation contract. You may have been told you will never have to face another fight with the devil or see another storm when you gave your life to Jesus. That's not so, my friend. This text is just one of many that presume an attack on the people of God. But God is a God who surrounds you and, therefore, can see the attack and the attackers. Nothing comes into your life that God does not allow. There is always going to be some kind of gap where the enemy can come in.

When you got saved and came out of your wilderness and onto Mount Zion, the enemy did not forget the path through which you came. When you got saved, the devil did not throw away your file. He keeps it updated, and he looks for every chance to attack you. But God doesn't just let him attack at will. God determines the timing, direction, and the perimeters of the attack. He controls the intensity and the duration of it. He has to sign off on all aspects of the attack before it ever touches you. That's why His Word says you will never face anything that you can't handle, because He not only knows everything about you,

He knows everything about what you're going to face. The enemy has to get permission from God to attack you. So know that whenever Satan gets to you, it's because God allowed him to, or God told him to. God only allows an attack that would ultimately benefit you, bring you closer to Him.

James said, "Count it all joy when you fall into various trials, knowing that the testing of your faith produces patience. But let patience have its perfect work, that you may be perfect and complete, lacking nothing" (James 1:2–4). God allows us to go through trials to grow us into the godly men and women He has called us to be. Still, He does promise that an attack will only continue for so long. God has already determined that, at a specific point in time, the attack will stop.

Though the enemy may knock you down, God's promise is that he will never knock you out. He may hold you down, but he won't keep you down. He cannot cancel your destiny. His attack will not eliminate your assignment or negate your anointing. It will hit you, but it won't rest on you. It's like a policeman wearing a bulletproof vest. When he gets shot, it doesn't mean that he won't get stunned or fall down. In fact, sometimes he does fall down and even appears to be dead. But if you keep watching, in a minute he'll get up. Because he was wearing the protective armor, the bullet took him down, but it didn't take him out.

The permissive will of God can allow an attack, even if you're righteous. Look at Job. The Bible says one day God was having a staff meeting, more or less, and in walked the devil. (He always comes around when God gets His people together.) God said, "Hey, devil, where've you been?" The devil said, "Oh, I've been to and fro in the earth." God said, "Really. Well, have you checked out my boy Job? He's pretty impressive, isn't he?" The devil said, "He's all right. He's a pretty straight dude. Of course,

I can't really get to him since you've got that protective hedge around him. Take it away and let me at him. When I get through with your godly boy, he'll curse you to your face!" God said, "You got it. Shoot your best shot. You can do anything but kill him" (Job 1:1–12, paraphrased). God set the perimeters and gave Satan permission to attack Job.

Round 1: Satan Attacked His Possessions
The Bible says the enemy attacked Job. In a matter of hours Job lost everything he had: his children were gone; his cattle were gone; and his wealth was gone.

Round 2: Satan Took His Health
Boils and sores broke out from the top of Job's head to the very bottom of his feet. His entire body was wrapped in disease.

Round 3: Satan Attacked His Reputation and His Marriage
Job's friends told him he must've ticked off God for all this to be happening. They didn't believe Job when he told them that was not the case. Then his wife went crazy on him. The man was broke and sick, and his wife told him to curse God and die. His wife, with whom he was one, turned on him and his God and told him to give in to the devil. Let me say here, that of all the things Satan did to Job, this was probably the worst. When a man and a woman marry, the Bible says they become one. Job's wife turning on him was akin to Job turning on himself.

Of course, at the end of the story, Job had a clearer picture of who God is and had a better relationship with Him. Everything Satan took from him was restored and then some. But what I want you to see is this. First, Job was a better man because of the attack on his life. He may have said afterward, "I thought I knew you, Lord, but not as well as I know you now." Secondly, God controlled everything from the very beginning. He knew just how much Job could take before the pressure of the attack would cause him to turn against God.

The Bible says the enemy was going to and fro, to and fro, and finally got to Job because God let him. Stop for a moment and remember that the word *trust* means "to attach oneself to." Remember also that God is Mount Scopus. He sees everything that happens in your life. Now look at 2 Chronicles 16:9: "For the eyes of the LORD run to and fro throughout the whole earth, to show Himself strong on behalf of those whose heart is loyal to Him."

To and fro. Where was the devil going? To and fro. Where are God's eyes? To and fro. The devil goes to and fro. God goes to and fro. If the devil could, he'd do his dirt when God wasn't looking. But he can't, because when God tossed him out of heaven, He restricted Satan's movement on the earth to "to and fro." What do you know, that's just the way God's eyes move. Satan can't go anywhere that God doesn't see him.

Scripture says that God is looking for somebody He can "show Himself strong" for. The word for "to show Himself strong" means "to attach to, or to be bound to firmly for the purpose of strengthening or supporting." God says, "If I can find somebody whose heart is right, I will attach Myself to that person." In other words, if God can find somebody who is attaching himself to Him because he is confident that he can rely on Him, then God will attach Himself in such a way that He will be everything that person thinks He is. He will confirm that person's confidence in Him. God's eyes move to and fro in the earth. He's looking for somebody to say, "I believe You, Lord. I believe You can take care of me." He's looking for you to say to the enemy, "I'm with God, and He can take you." As soon as you make up your mind that you're with God, He's with you.

The course of godliness should take you on the pathway of maturity. And with God as your protector, no one will be able to keep you from your destination. God will be there to see to it.

Prayer
for
Godly Perspective

Holy Father who sees all, I thank You for Your
    eyes that see me wherever I am.
Lord, teach me how to attach myself to You.
Give me the confidence to let go of worldly
    security and cling to You.
Show me the truth of who You are, and give me
    the power to walk in that truth, unmoved
    by the attack of the enemy.
Show me Your goodness, that I might emulate
    it.
Point my heart toward You.
Set my affections on things above.
Remind me that there is nothing that happens
    in my life that is not under Your control,
    so that I may rejoice in my tribulation.
May I always remember that You are worthy of
    glory, honor, praise, and adulation,
    regardless of my circumstances.
In Jesus' name, Amen.

Chapter 9 Exercises

Exercise 1: The Journey to Mt. Zion

1. Memorize Psalm 125:1: "Those who trust in the LORD / Are like Mount Zion, / Which cannot be moved, but abides forever."

2. The journey to Mount Zion, as described in Psalm 125, is a symbol of the believer's ascent to spiritual maturity. Israel first stopped at Mount Sinai, where Moses received the revelation of God's Word. But revelation is not an end unto itself. Revelation is always the beginning of a journey to relationship. Think about how Mount Zion represents relationship in your life.

3. The people of Zion, or the believer on his way to spiritual maturity, is marked by certain character traits. Think about how these traits apply to your life:

- He attaches himself to the Lord;
- His life reflects the goodness of the Lord; and
- His heart is set on the Lord.

4. God's goal is to establish us as Mount Zion. He promises to make each of us unmovable. The picture is painted in more detail in Psalm 121:3, where it is said that the Lord "will not allow your foot to be moved." Can you think of an instance in your life when this happened?

5. The view of Zion represents God's eye on us. From where He sits on Mount Scopus, He can see everything going on in our lives. Does this make you feel more secure, or do you feel insecure because you're hiding something from the Lord?

Exercise 2: To Know Him Is to Know Him

The process of God is to tell us something about Himself or His nature, then give us an opportunity to believe He is what He says He is. For example, He may tell you that He is faithful. But He won't stop there. He'll put you in a position to believe Him for something incredible and miraculous, something eyes have not seen, but something your heart yearns for. Then methodically, systematically, from glory to glory, He'll bring it to pass, specifically what you expected, but exceeding abundantly above all you could ask or think. Following are some things God tells us about Himself in His Word. Write specifically how He has shown Himself to be those things in your life. If you have not experienced a particular trait, write a prayer asking Him to further reveal Himself to you. Everyone should, at least, have something to write for Faithful. If He has shown you anything else, He has proven Himself faithful to do it.

Faithful:

_____

_____

Comforter:

_____

_____

Healer:

_____

_____

Father:

_____

_____

Ever Present:

_____

_____

Merciful:

_____

_____

Truth:

_____

_____

Protector:

_____

_____

Provider:

_____

_____

Exercise 3: The View from up There

Psalm 139 overwhelms me sometimes because it speaks of the very core of God's love for us. He sees us. He's with us. He's in us in our past, present, and future. He's even with our thoughts before they enter our minds. He's in all those places . . . and He loves us in all those places, at the same time, all the time.

Read Psalm 139:1–18. Then meditate on its parts. Let the Holy Spirit minister to you by giving you a more complete understanding of a loving, ever-present God. Don't move on to another verse until the Holy Spirit is finished moving in you. I've paraphrased each verse to extract the meaning for you.

v. 2—God knows every move of my body and my mind.

v. 3—He plotted the course of my life and tells me where and how to walk and when to rest.

v. 4—He knows what I'm going to say before I say it. He also understands what I say and why I said it.

v. 5—Wherever I go, His hand is on me. He is where I've been and where I will be.

v. 6—A true understanding of the height, depth, and breadth of God's presence is beyond me. As far as my imagination will take me is not far enough to encompass Him.

v. 7—There isn't any place I can go where God can't be touched or felt.

v. 8—He is even in the places I can't reach in my mortality— like heaven or hell.

vv. 9–10—If I go to unknown places, I might be lost, but He isn't. He guides me, even when I don't know where I am.

v. 11—I can't choose to hide from Him. Nothing can be hidden from God.

v. 12—Nothing can obscure His sight. To Him what's in the dark is as visible as what's in the light.

v. 13—He was guiding my life and protecting me before I was born.

v. 15—He knew what I would look like before I was conceived. He formed me.

v. 16—Every moment of every day of my life is already recorded in His book, and has been since before I took my first breath.

vv. 17–18 He's with me always, thinking about me always, and knowing how He has loved me always.

Chapter 10

The Course of Godliness, Part 2: Going the Way of Christ

Those who trust in the LORD
Are like Mount Zion,
Which cannot be moved, but abides forever.
As the mountains surround Jerusalem,
So the LORD surrounds His people
From this time forth and forever.

Psalm 125:1–2

The psalmist says that the godly man and woman shall be as Mount Zion and that God will surround them with His presence and protection as Zion is surrounded with mountains. The most prominent range of the mountains surrounding Zion, or Jerusalem, is the Mount of Olives. It is just to the east of Jerusalem and runs north and south. It is the most traveled of the mountain ranges around Jerusalem. In fact, it is impossible to come into Jerusalem without coming through the Mount of Olives. The road to Jerusalem comes up the side of the hill of the Mount of Olives, goes down across the Kidron Valley, then up another hill to Jerusalem.

Jesus traveled that road many times. Often he would stop in the city of Bethany, just next to the Mount of Olives, to visit His friends Martha and Lazarus, whom He raised from the dead. Bethany is on the way to Zion, about two-thirds of the way up. Jesus often made stops there, as well, to rest or to minister to his friends. Sometimes He taught informally. Mary, the sister of Martha, sat at Jesus' feet and listened as He told her of His Father, their Father in heaven, and His plans for them on earth. The road to Jerusalem was never a straight shot. There were always stops, necessary stops, along the way.

Consider our spiritual journey as the road to Zion. Consider also, that like Jesus, we are not expected to make that journey without stopping to serve others, to minister, and to be ministered to. Sometimes, we're expected to rest. The stops on the way to Zion are many and varied, but their purpose is singular. The goal of every stop on the way to spiritual maturity is growth. Each place you visit is designed to better equip you for your next step, whatever that step may be.

The Mount of Olives was named for the olive trees that cover it. Olive oil was used for many things, but particularly in anointing ceremonies. Olive oil in Scripture is symbolic of the Holy Spirit. As we make stops on the Mount of Olives in our spiritual journey, we are given a fresh anointing of God's Holy Spirit to equip us for the next level of God's purpose for us. As I said, you cannot get to Jerusalem without going through the Mount of Olives. You cannot grow spiritually without periodic infusions of the Holy Spirit to energize you and enable you to do what God has called you to do.

Now, there is also a valley that separates the Mount of Olives from the ascent to Jerusalem. This valley is unavoidable. It is called the Kidron Valley. *Kidron* means "turbid," which is defined as "thick or opaque from sediment, muddy or obscure." Likewise, in every spiritual journey toward godliness, there are valleys. These are places where the way is unclear. Valleys are places of confusion for the child of God. Picture a jar of water with a layer of sand at the bottom. If you were to put your hand in the jar and stir up the contents, the water becomes disturbed.

What was once clear water is now opaque. That is the valley for the believer. Our lives are stirred up to the point of confusion. We are not blind, but we cannot see because the way is hidden from us.

These are places where you feel you can't go any lower. Places that make you long for the higher ground, the spots of clarity, rest, growth, and fellowship with other saints. Spiritual valleys are unavoidable. Moreover, God ordains them as a testing ground for the faith He has built in you to that point. But God never requires us to take a step that He has not prepared us for, or that He has not taken Himself.

Lessons in the Garden of Gethsemane

In Mark 14:26 and 32 we read: "And when they had sung a hymn, they went out to the Mount of Olives . . . Then they came to a place which was named Gethsemane; and He said to His disciples, 'Sit here, while I pray.'"

On the way to Jerusalem, just before you reach the Kidron Valley, is a garden at the base of the Mount of Olives. This is the Garden of Gethsemane, the most important stop Jesus made on His way to Calvary. *Gethsemane* is a word that means "oil press"—the place of pressing or squeezing, the place where God presses out of you all of the oil, or anointing, He put into you.

There are lessons you must learn in the garden of Gethsemane if you're going to be a godly man or godly woman. There are things that God wants to teach you in the Gethsemane classroom that you can't learn anyplace else. Going through Gethsemane is not an optional extra in your spiritual walk. It is required. Not only is it required, but it is the only way to prepare you for the valley ahead.

A Lesson in Loneliness

We read in Luke 22:39–41: "Coming out, He went to the Mount of Olives, as He was accustomed, and His disciples also followed Him. When He came to the place, He said to them, 'Pray that you may not enter into temptation.' And He was withdrawn from them about a stone's throw, and He knelt down and prayed."

Jesus went with the disciples to the garden. He told them to wait, then He went off alone to a different section of the garden area. The Bible says He came with them and then He withdrew from them. Jesus was in the garden with the group, but by Himself. Do you know what it's like to be in a place with a crowd of people all around you, yet you feel you're alone? I promise you, if you want to be a man or woman of God, you are going to have to learn something about loneliness. You're going to learn about standing alone. You're going to learn about being in a place where you feel separated, divided, withdrawn, and segregated from everybody around you.

If you're going to grow to spiritual maturity—reach mountain status with God, you're going to experience days, seasons, times, and phases when you will stand all by yourself. I don't care who your parents are, how close you and your parents are, how close you and your husband or wife are, or how many loving children you have. I don't care how long you've been in fellowship with the saints, how popular you are, or how cute or educated you are. I don't care what fraternity or sorority you're in, how rich or poor you are, or how spiritually deep you are. You're going to have to learn how to stand by yourself.

It is in this garden of Gethsemane that you learn the value in loneliness and what God is trying to tell you. There are some things that God wants to speak into your life and into your spirit. Things you will never hear in a crowd. There are times when

God wants to commune and fellowship with just you. If you don't pull away from the crowd when God has a word for you, you will hear so many voices that you won't be able to distinguish which of them is God's.

There are times when you have to stand in the very presence of God and have Him meet you in your place of loneliness and despair. When He meets you, there will be issues that you deal with in this season of godliness that you cannot share even with the people who love you.

A season of loneliness does not mean that you're in sin or that God is mad or that He's turned His back on you. There are things that you will go through that others around you, no matter how much they love you or how well they know you, cannot and will not relate to. The disciples couldn't even relate. Jesus told them to stay there and pray. He called a prayer meeting and then left to pray. You will discover, if you read back a little way, that Jesus set this up earlier in the upper room when He told them He was going to Calvary. He told them He was going to die. You get a sense that He wanted them to pray for Him, and yet He didn't hang around for the prayer meeting. He went off by Himself to pray, and the disciples went to sleep. They could not relate. Jesus was a stone's throw away, praying, crying, and sweating blood, while the disciples, who said they loved Him and knew He was Christ and would never leave Him, were a stone's throw away, sleeping! Some of the hardest times in your life will be faced with the people closest to you, and they may be unaware that you're going through them. You'll find yourself crying in the middle of the night with nobody to call. Some of you will be married, lying next to somebody, and still have nobody to call.

The lesson of loneliness is Gethsemane's gift to that person who finds his or her security in things or people rather than in

God. Friendship with the world makes us enemies of God. Loneliness is that pain that separates us from our earthly ties and forces us to cling to One who said He would never leave us or forsake us.

A Lesson in a Crisis of Will

We read in Mark 14:35–36: "He went a little farther, and fell on the ground, and prayed that if it were possible, the hour might pass from Him. And He said, 'Abba, Father, all things are possible for You. Take this cup away from Me.'"

There is not another scene in the entire life of Jesus that more vividly manifests His humanity than this one. We find Him in the garden trying to bargain with God. I was in Jerusalem near the praying wall, and there were hundreds of people out there in the courtyard. In the center of the court, there was a little boy around four or five. He was crying, "Abba! Abba!" *Abba* means "daddy." When Jesus called upon the Father, He said, "Abba." It is a term of endearment. It speaks of intimacy. In essence, he was saying, "Daddy, with You all things are possible. Lord, I know that You are the Creator. You are the Father of Abraham, Isaac, and Jacob. I know that You're the God who parted the Red Sea. I know that You're the God who met Daniel in the den of lions. You met the Hebrew boys in the furnace. You are the God who can do everything. And by the way, Lord, would You mind cutting me some slack? Will you let this cup pass from me?"

Have you ever bargained with God? Have you ever asked God for a Plan B? God, I would do so much better with a multiple-choice test. Give me a chance, please? I want you to see in this that God is real. He doesn't play games with you. He doesn't paint some pie-in-the-sky, everything's-coming-up-roses type picture of godliness. He lets you know the reality of the struggle and that there are going to be times when your flesh will struggle with your spirit. This is part of your humanity, and you are not unspiritual because you wrestle with God's will for your life. The Bible says Jesus did.

You will never be the man or woman God wants you to be until you learn the reality of the crisis of will. Now, I'm not talking about disobedience. That's when God tells you to do something and you make a choice to do something else. As I said earlier, most of us are educated far beyond our obedience. We know more than we do. We could spend the rest of our lives doing what God has already told us to do. But the reality of the Christian life is that we come to places where there is a tension and a crisis of the will. There are places where it's not an issue of not wanting to move, but feeling paralyzed to the point of being unable to move. At this point we ask God to give us another option. Keep in mind, Jesus wanted to fulfill God's purpose. He just wanted to take another route to do it. Contrast this with the story of Jonah, who didn't want to do what God told him and chose to go in another direction on his own. That is sin. A crisis of will is not sin. How we handle that crisis is where the potential for sin lies.

A Lesson in Betrayal

We read in Luke 22:47: "And while He was still speaking, behold, a multitude; and he who was called Judas, one of the twelve, went before them and drew near to Jesus to kiss Him."

Luke said Judas went before them and drew himself near Jesus and kissed Him. Mark said Jesus prayed on His way to Calvary. Then in comes a crowd of people, mostly soldiers, led by a brother named Judas. Mark said that when Judas came to Jesus, he said, "Master, Master," and then he kissed Him. The road to godliness makes a stop at Gethsemane where every godly man and woman learns to deal with the reality of betrayal.

A friend betrayed Jesus. I don't think I know of any man or woman of God, who is truly strong in the Lord, who cannot look back at some chapter in his or her life and see betrayal by a loved one.

The Bible says Judas came and called Him Master. This was an endearing term that disciples used. The relationship between disciple and rabbi was a very strong bond. Judas was a man who came to Jesus behind a facade of love. In fact, if you go back and read it, you will discover that they had just left the upper room. Jesus had come in and realized that there was no servant. So the Bible says He got down on his knees, wrapped a towel around Himself, and began to wash the feet of the disciples. He washed Judas's feet. He had just blessed Judas. And now, the one whom He blessed betrayed Him.

I would not have you deceived into thinking that this road to godliness is some kind of utopia where you just put your hand in Jesus' hand and march on up to Zion with your brothers and sisters without a care in the world. Like Jesus, God requires you to learn something about being hurt by someone who loves you, by someone you love, and by someone who says he loves you. You will learn something about betrayal from people you have blessed, people you have helped, people to whom you gave your time and substance.

But all things work together for good. The blessing of betrayal is the gift of forgiveness. Forgiveness is God's response to the betrayal of sin, which is our heritage from the Garden of Eden. Betrayal is turning your back on a relationship. We do that with every act of disobedience, every act of sin. Jesus carried the wounds and bruises of our transgressions against God. Forgiveness is the healing of relationship. It not only mends the heart of the one betrayed, but it can also restore the one whose diseased heart committed the act of betrayal.

A Lesson in Restraint

We read in Luke 22:49–51:

> When those around Him saw what was going to happen, they said to Him, "Lord, shall we strike with the sword?" And one of them struck the servant of the high priest and cut off his right ear.

> But Jesus answered and said, "Permit even this." And He touched his ear and healed him.

When they came to arrest Jesus, the disciples asked Him if they should fight. Then, without waiting for an answer, one of them, probably Peter, pulled out a sword and cut off an ear of one of the soldiers. Now if he was aiming to cut the man's ear off, he would have struck downward with the knife and cut him on the shoulder as well, or at least his shoulder blade. But Scripture says all he got was an ear. This implies that he swung the sword, the guy ducked, and all he got was an ear. My point is that whoever swung the sword was trying to cut somebody's head off! So Jesus, the only cool head in the bunch, picks up the ear, reattaches it, and heals it.

Along the road to godliness, one of the lessons you must learn is the lesson of restraint. Jesus had the power to destroy all of them, yet He displayed spiritual discipline, strength, and mercy.

The road to godliness makes a stop in Gethsemane to teach you how not to use the very power that God has given you. God is able to providentially orchestrate a set of circumstances so that the very people who would harm you will end up being at the mercy of your power and authority. When you hold all the cards, one of the lessons of godliness is to learn when not to use that power. By signing your name, you could take everything someone has. Just one word from you could cost somebody his job. Your say-so could destroy somebody's reputation. Jesus could have wiped everybody out, but He chose not to. He restrained Himself.

There are going to be times in this walk with God that you really want to get somebody back for what they did to you. God will teach you how to show that person mercy by showing you how much mercy He's given you. Some of you are in bondage to your ex-boyfriend or girlfriend or your ex-spouse. You're a prisoner of your past. Sure, you've been betrayed. I know your heart is broken. You've been walked all over. But be careful. God may put you in a position where you actually have an opportunity to get revenge.

The person who has learned the lesson of restraint at Gethsemane will lay aside bitterness and build a new life in the power of the Holy Ghost. Know that you have bigger fish to fry and bigger blessings to catch. You've got to claim the power that God gives you to show some mercy, so God can then bless you and take you to another level of growth. Those same people who betrayed you will get paranoid. They'll look over their shoulder and wait for you to drop the other shoe. But here you are, wearing a new pair of shoes and walking on in Jesus' name. You don't have to get revenge. God says vengeance is His department. You don't have time for revenge. You've got a race to run. You've got a destiny to reach. You've got a crown to claim.

Spiritual restraint is not weakness. It is meekness. Meekness is power under control. As I look back on my own life, I see how God has blessed me with a perfect portrait of holy restraint. In 1977, I was working at a radio station in Hollywood, doing very well, when God called me into the ministry. (Actually, I was called long before that, but 1977 was the year I chose to acknowledge it.) I quit my job at the station so I could go to school to prepare for ministry.

I remember praying, "Lord, I'm really not too big on doing this thing, but if you really want me to, I will. I'll jump into this with both feet." A dear pastor friend of mine said, "Man, I think you're messing up. Your wife is going to leave you. You just got married, you're doing well, and you're going to quit your job? You and your wife are used to living a certain lifestyle, and you're going to go to school with no income. I'm going to pray for you, man, because she is going to leave you." He was not trying to be funny. He was serious. This was a dear friend whom I trusted, and he told me I was making the biggest mistake of my life. He thought he'd had a revelation. He tried to save his friend.

That phone call plagued me. There were times when I didn't know where the next dime was coming from. There were times when I would travel somewhere to preach and would get nothing. There were times when I had no money coming in, and that phone call echoed in my ear. Here I am, the man of the house, king of my castle, and I can't even put food on the table. That set of circumstances had been divinely orchestrated so that my wife had the power to destroy me. Wives, be careful what you say about a man's income or his job. We think we are what we do. My wife had the power in her hand to destroy me. One raised eyebrow, one off-color comment, one conversation with one of her friends that got back to me, and I would have been devastated. But not one time did she turn away from me. I was at my weakest, and God used that woman to build me up. She'd tell me I could get strong. Because she was with me, I walked like I had money. I may not have had a dime in my pocket, but I had a million-dollar woman on my arm!

Sometimes God will put you in a position where people who could destroy you will bless you because they've got so much God in them. They will hold you up until you can stand up.

A Lesson in Nevertheless

We read in Luke 22:42: "Father if it is Your will, take this cup away from Me; nevertheless . . ." You cannot leave Gethsemane without learning the lesson of nevertheless. Nevertheless means, "Lord, I'll do it and I'll do it Your way because that's what You want." Nevertheless means "Lord, I don't really want to do this, but what You want matters more to me than what I don't want. So let's go." Nevertheless is an act of your will that submits to His will. It's when you really don't want to love that woman the way Christ loved the church, but nevertheless . . . It's when you don't want to do good to those that spitefully use you, but nevertheless . . .

Nevertheless means choosing God's agenda over your agenda. In the spirit realm, the time between this verse and the next verse is a twinkling of an eye. Verse 42 says, "Nevertheless not my will, but Yours, be done." Verse 43 says: "Then an angel appeared to Him from heaven, strengthening Him." The text implies this happened all of a sudden. It does not say an angel came to strengthen him. It says an angel came strengthening Him. That means that while the angel was on his way, he was already strengthening Him. So, when he got there, Jesus was already stronger in the Holy Ghost.

The road to godliness cannot be traveled without learning how to access divine assistance. When you've gone as far as you can go, you've got to learn how to call on Abba Father. And the moment you say, "Lord, I cannot handle this," He dispatches an angel. The Bible says angels are ministering spirits, which means they are spirits that move only on assignment. So when you as a child of God say, "Nevertheless," God sends one specially trained angel to aid you with your trial. While he's coming, he's giving you the strength to do what God has called you to do.

The Exodus from Gethsemane

When you come out of Gethsemane, your place of loneliness, you don't come out by yourself. When you have been betrayed and have had your heart broken, you don't step out of that mess by yourself. God says He's got angels who are coming to strengthen you. When you step out with the angel nobody can see, all people know is that the last time they saw you, you were down in the dumps. The last time they saw you, you were broken and dejected. The last time they saw you, you had tears streaming down your face. But when they see you now, they can't see your angel. They want an explanation for why you look so good today, when you looked so broken up yesterday.

When Jesus went up a hill called Calvary, He had some angels. When He went to the cross, He had some angels. When they put Him in a tomb, we know He had some angels, because early Sunday morning when He stepped out of that grave, those same angels opened the door. The Bible says God sent an angel to roll away the stone, and out stepped Jesus with all power in heaven and earth in His hands. God's encouragement to you today is: "You've been lonely long enough. You've been crying long enough. You've got some angels on the way. It's time for you to come out of your place of Gethsemane. Come out with your angels, and whatever is waiting for you, you and your angel can handle it. Whatever the devil throws your way, you and your angel will catch it and deal with it."

Maybe you've never been in Gethsemane. I've been there. I've been as down as I could be. I've been so down, I had to reach up to touch down. But when I reached up, God reached down. He reached down and picked me up. God will meet you in your garden of loneliness, frustration, confusion, distress, struggle, and trial. And He'll meet you there with an angel specifically assigned to help bring you out.

Prayer
for
Perseverance

Abba Father, I know You take us through trials
    to strengthen us.
I know that whatever way You take us through
    a trial is the best and only way we could
    have gone.
When I am lonely, remind me that You are my
    comfort.
When I feel betrayed and mistreated, give me a
    heart of forgiveness and show me how to
    put away my bitterness.
When I struggle with Your will for my life, give
    me the words to cry out to You.
And when I cry out to You, Father, I thank You
    now for the angel You will send to my aid.
I am so thankful for Your love, Heavenly
    Father.
Show me how to love You more.
In Jesus' name, Amen.

Chapter 10 Exercises

Exercise 1: Stops on the Road to Zion
   1. Memorize Psalm 125:2:

As the mountains surround Jerusalem,
So the LORD surrounds His people
From this time forth and forever.

   2. Sometimes there are stops on the road to Zion. Likewise there are stops on the road of our spiritual walk with God. There are stops to minister and to be ministered unto by others. There is rest or struggle. Sometimes we wait for direction, instruction, or provision. The goal of every stop on the way to Zion prepares us for the next step in the journey. In your spiritual walk is growth the goal of every stop?

   3. Gethsemane is a garden at the base of the Mount of Olives. The name means "oil press." There are lessons God teaches us during the press of our Gethsemane experience. These include lessons in loneliness, betrayal, the crisis of the will, restraint, and the lesson of nevertheless. Can you find instances in your life when you've been pressed?

Exercise 2: Gethsemane
   Three of the four gospels recount Jesus' experience in the Garden of Gethsemane. Each of them teaches us a different lesson about our relationship with God and the preparation for purpose.
   Read Mark 14:32–42.

1. Describe how Jesus felt. Can you remember a time when you might have felt like He did?

_____

_____

_____

2. *Abba* is a term of endearment that means "father," or more accurately, "daddy." When you pray, how do you see God? What kind of father is He to you? How do you see His personality, mood, demeanor, expression, attitude, and disposition toward you? How consistent is your perception with Scripture?

_____

_____

_____

Exercise 3: Comparing Scriptures

Read Matthew 26:36–46.

1. Mark 14:39 says Jesus went away and "spoke the same words." Matthew's account confirms that they were the same basic words, but there was a different attitude. There is a shift in Christ's mindset. Compare Matthew 26:39 and Mark 14:42. What is the shift?

_____

_____

_____

2. Have you ever adjusted, or fine-tuned, your prayers as God's will became progressively clearer to you?

_____

_____

_____

Now read Luke 22:39–46. We know that Jesus prayed a total of three times. Here we see that something happened between the second and third prayers. Jesus' heart had moved to a place of clarity, understanding, and acceptance of God's will. Look at God's response to Him.

3. What happens in verses 43–44?

_____

_____

_____

4. Jesus was strengthened by the angel of the Lord. Then the Word says He was in agony. That word *agony* refers to "an intense fear which trembles in the face of a particular issue, but allows you to remain and face it." Has God ever given you something to do that scared you, but later He gave you the strength to stand and face it?

_____

_____

_____

Notice that the way Jesus stood and faced His fear was to "pray more earnestly." Also, it's important to note that it is not a sin to be afraid. Paul tells Timothy that God did not give us a spirit of fear. That is true. But many take that to mean that being afraid is a sin. But Jesus was sinless.

Fear can be a catalyst for sin if we allow it to be. Fear can make you doubt God and that is the sin of unbelief. Fear can make you run away from what God has called you to do. Disobedience is sin. Fear of rejection can cause you to hurt someone's feelings or act with pride. Jesus was afraid, but He didn't let His fear keep Him from seeking and being obedient to the will of God.

5. How do you handle fear?

_____

_____

_____

Exercise 4: Other Lessons

1. Has a friend ever betrayed you?
2. Have you ever had the power to hurt someone and chosen not to?
3. Have you ever wanted to say no to God?
4. Have you ever denied yourself and your own desires and said "nevertheless" to God?

Think about each of these questions. Then shift the angle of your perspective and answer them again.

5. Have you ever betrayed God?
6. Has God ever been merciful to you?
7. Have you ever asked God for something that He didn't want to give you?
8. Has God ever denied Himself for you?

Chapter 11
Contentment in Godliness

For I have learned in whatever state I am, to be content.
Philippians 4:11

The Bible says that godliness is profitable, gainful, and useful—not just in this life but in the life to come. God has called us to live godly lives, lives that express the truth of who He is. I had become quite comfortable with that as I studied this concept of godliness. Then in 1 Timothy 6:6, Paul threw me a curve (as he often does) that hit me right between my spiritual eyes. There Paul revealed an aspect of godliness, I must admit, I had never thought about. Our definition of godliness is consistent conduct that is consistent with the character of God. But Paul suggested that godliness has a partner. In fact, he went so far as to say godliness is not all it can be without this holy associate. First Timothy 6:6 says: "Now godliness with contentment is great gain."

Godliness with contentment. Contentment is not one of those concepts you hear too much about. You don't find too many people dancing and shouting over contentment. Very few praise parties are thrown around contentment. Yet the Word says godliness with contentment is gain, even great gain. As if that weren't enough, as you go on and read the broader context of 1 Timothy 6, you discover that primarily it is talking about financial contentment. The gain Paul talked about is the idea of procuring riches or becoming prosperous materially. He sought to set aright the doctrine of false teachers who sought gain and so justified their greed by defining and describing gain as a measure of God's favor. He spoke against and stood against these teachers who determined that the blessing hand of God was seen primarily in financial terms. Go back to 1 Timothy 6:5: "Useless wranglings of men of corrupt minds and destitute of the truth, who suppose that godliness is a means of gain. From such withdraw yourself."

Notice how he describes these dear brethren. They are men of corrupt minds, and they are destitute of the truth, which means there is no semblance, reasonable facsimile, or shred of truth in supposing that financial gain is a measure of godliness. In other words, that doctrine of gain as godliness is nowhere near the truth. And yet, it was quite popular with the believers of the day. But Paul's word to these believers was to withdraw themselves from those teachers and that doctrine. Then he gave them the correct perspective of godliness as it relates to prosperity. He says godliness with contentment is great gain. That is prosperity. That is wealth. The godly man or woman who is content is rich.

Let me say right here that Paul was in no way deifying poverty. He was not declaring that being poor somehow makes a person godlier than one who has or aspires to wealth. As a matter of fact, that doctrine of thought that proposes that godliness meant having nothing was also spread by some other ascetic groups in Paul's day. So there were two opposing philosophies of the time. One said that true godliness was measured by how much stuff you had, and on the other extreme was the idea that true godliness was measured by how much stuff you didn't have. The latter group lived up in the mountains in caves and owned no material possessions. But Paul said godliness with contentment was great gain.

That's a word for those of you climbing the corporate ladder, who have so completely bought into the system of the times that says the Golden Rule is: He who has the gold rules. The off-spring of that philosophy is self-centeredness, selfishness, and self-glorification. This is the "me" generation, where *I* is the first and last letter of the alphabet and every letter in between. Our country is a population of one, our flag is a mirror, and our national anthem is "My Way." For many of us, when Paul said "godliness with contentment is great gain," what we hear is "godliness with great gain is contentment." So we get all we can, can all we get, sit on the lid, and burn the rest of it.

Unfortunately this mercenary viewpoint finds both societal and theological support. Inside and outside the church, a person's worth to others is often defined by his or her material worth. And that personal worth is too often the gauge by which we evaluate a person's value to God and His kingdom. If you have a car and the next guy has a bus pass, you obviously have more favor with God than he does. On the other hand, if you have a Ford and he has a Lexus, it must mean that God is more favorably disposed toward him. The principle is that gain and material gathering is a definition and a manifestation of godliness. But Paul hits us squarely between the eyes and says that's not so. You want to be rich? Be godly and content.

For Richer or Poorer

Paul was not extolling the virtues of poverty, nor was he denouncing riches. Look at what he says in 1 Timothy 6:17: "Command those who are rich in this present age not to be haughty, nor to trust in uncertain riches but in the living God, who gives us richly all things to enjoy."

Warn the rich, exhort them, and charge them so they don't

get high-minded. Riches are not a source of arrogance, because it is the living God who gives us all things. Whatever you have came from God. The writer of Chronicles says even when we give, we give out of God's hand, right back into His hand, because all that we have comes from God. When we give, we are simply asking God how much of what He has allowed us to control would He now have us give back to Him as an expression of our gratitude to Him. We're just giving God what belongs to Him anyway. He was just kind enough to let us use it.

So contentment comes when we understand that God takes care of everything that belongs to Him. Since all I have belongs to Him, and I belong to Him, I rest in the assurance that He's taking care of my stuff and me because it's all His anyway. Wealth then ceases to be a goal or a source of arrogance, because the truth of the matter is no matter how much money we have or things we've accumulated, we have no real possessions. So even those who are rich should be careful not to get too full of themselves. Why? Look at 1 Timothy 6:9–10: "But those who desire to be rich fall into temptation and a snare, and into many foolish and harmful lusts which drown men in destruction and perdition. For the love of money is a root of all kinds of evil."

This is one of the most misquoted verses in Scripture. It does not say money is the root of all evil. It says the love of money is the root of all evil. So Paul warns those who have a lot of it to be careful lest they be tempted. The temptation is twofold. First, there is the temptation to assume that you deserve what you've got because of who you are, not whose you are. The second temptation is to hoard what you have. Rather than being a channel of blessings, you turn around and become a reservoir. The purpose of wealth is, in part, to be a channel of blessings. Paul said in 1 Timothy 6:18 that the rich shouldn't be too caught up in what they have and that they should "do good, that they be rich in good works, ready to give, willing to share." Be mindful that there are tricks and traps that the enemy has laid specifically for folks who have money. But God never says get rid of your money, just beware of its temptation.

But then, you have to beware of the temptations that come with everything. There is also a temptation that comes with poverty. If you're not careful, you'll be tempted to think that God doesn't like you anymore, or that he likes someone else better than you. Or you'll be tempted to covet what others have to the point that you can't get your mind off of money, despite the fact that you don't have any. Don't be fooled, some of the biggest lovers of money are the people who don't have any. Jesus had much to say on the subject of money. In Luke 12:15 He said, "Take heed and beware of covetousness, for one's life does not consist in the abundance of the things he possesses."

This kind of sums it up, doesn't it? Jesus said the essence of your life is not in what you possess. The car you drive does not define you. The house you live in does not define you. You are not defined by what you own. Don't define yourself by what you have rather than who you are, or by what you can get rather than whose you are. If you do this, your godliness cannot be all that it should be, because your conduct will not reflect the character of the God who says your life is not your possessions.

For Better or Worse

Contentment is not circumstance-dependent. It does not wait to see if it's sunny outside before it puts on a smile. Paul said to the Philippians that he had learned to be content regardless of his circumstances. Contentment is not a statement about your situation. It is a statement about your sufficiency in your situation. Contentment says that whatever I have is enough. Now, don't confuse contentment with complacency. Contentment is grateful for where it is. Complacency is unsatisfied where it is. Contentment is hopeful; complacency is hopeless. Contentment always looks forward; complacency just looks around. Contentment says, "I can handle this because I can do all things." Complacency says, "I guess I'll deal with this since I don't have a choice." Contentment is gratitude; complacency is attitude. Complacency looks at circumstances and weeps. Contentment looks at the God of circumstances and rejoices.

Paul learned to be content wherever he was because he knew he was just passing through. Contentment never pitches a tent where it is. But it does take notes, so that if that situation comes around again, there will be no confusion. God brought me out last time; He'll bring me out this time. I've been here, and I've done this. I'm not going to pull my hair out, and I'm not going to go off the deep end. I'm not going to stay up all night walking the floors because I'm broke. If the truth were told, I've been broke before. The last time I was broke, I learned some things. Paul said he learned how to abase and abound. Some of us have learned how to abound, but haven't quite gotten the hang of abasement. You've learned what it's like to live high on the hog, but you haven't learned how to be in the hog's pen. I need to tell you that you don't have to go around looking for the hog pen. If you just keep on living, there are some hogs sniffing around right now trying to pull you in. Just in case you happened to fall in, Paul said, learn to be content there.

Paul learned how to be full and hungry. I know what it's like to have a lot of food on the table. I feel I've sinned against God by throwing away enough to feed three or four people. But I also remember a time when sardines and crackers were my dinner. Paul told me not to forget those days. At the very least I remember them enough to praise God that they've passed. I remember, in case I have to go back there, that I've learned some things.

Contentment is not just about being satisfied. It's about being sufficient. Contentment means realizing that God sees you where you are. It means not giving in to the sin of covetousness. One of the things that will keep you where you are longer is to wish your way out by wanting something someone else has. The reason some of you don't have a spouse right now is because you wish you had someone else's spouse. Jesus said beware of the sin of covetousness. Ungodliness is to covet that which someone else has.

Contentment doesn't just show up in you one day. Paul said he had to learn it. The word *learn* means "to learn something that can be revealed only through experience." This kind of knowledge comes only from experiencing something with God because the Holy Spirit teaches all things. Paul said he'd been through some things with God, and he'd learned some things about God. The things he learned about God gave him a sense of contentment about his circumstances, whatever those circumstances were. What are you fretting about today? What are you in a panic about this minute? What is it that you don't have that you are panicking about because you don't have it? What is that uneasiness you're feeling that makes contentment impossible?

The man or woman who is discontent can never be godly. The presence of discontent, by definition, means there is a lack of faith in the sufficiency of God. We talk about the salvation of God and the sovereignty of God, but we don't hear very much about the sufficiency of God. Paul said in Colossians 2:10, "You are complete in Him." Contentment is sufficiency. This means "I am complete in Christ, even though I may not have what I want to have in my life." I am complete in Him because He is sufficient for me. With Him, I can do all things—and being able to do all things is enough for me.

Do you find your sufficiency in Christ? As you look at your life up to this point—your career, your family, your friends, your finances—are you content?

To be content does not mean that you have no desire to progress or acquire things. To be content means that what you have is sufficient at this point in your life because you realize that God is a seasonal God. I can be content where I am because I know that there are cycles with God. Discontent comes when we conclude that the season that we're in is the season we will always be in. Then there is no reason for hope. If there is no hope, then we have no faith, because our faith is the substance of things hoped for. If there is no faith, we cannot please God. If we cannot please Him, God knows that we cannot be godly. God will never comfort us in the ungodliness of unbelief. Godliness tells us that God is a seasonal God.

Now, there is good news and bad news about the seasons of God. The bad news is you can miss your season. You can miss a season of blessing. Any number of sins can cause you to miss your season: covetousness and envy, ungodliness and unrighteousness, anger and bitterness, and unforgivingness. If the truth were told, some of us have missed a season or two. Some of us have missed a blessing or two as well.

But the good news is that if you keep on living, your season will come around again. Isn't God a good God? Some of us blew it. Some of us messed up. Some of us missed the season. Some of us let our summer season drift into the uncertainty of fall and then the bitter coldness of winter. But if you keep living, spring will follow the winter, and before you know it, you'll be back at summer again. Contentment is realizing I've got another summer coming. I've got another chance to harvest. It doesn't matter where I am now. Wherever I am, God has met me there and given me what I needed. In my contentment, I know that God is a God who says if I wait on Him, no matter where I am, I'll be all right.

I've learned how to go with nothing. I've been down to nothing. But when I didn't have a dime, I learned something. I learned that my God shall supply all my needs according to His riches. No one taught me that. I didn't get that from the prophets of old. I didn't get it from Abraham, Isaac, or Jacob. I didn't get it from the writings of David. Paul said it to me in Philippians 4:19, but I had to learn it on my own. I've been through some things. I've been through some storms. I've been through some hard times. I've been through some trials. I've been through some difficulties. I've had to climb some rough mountains. But I've learned that if I wait on the Lord long enough, I shall renew my strength. I will mount up with wings as eagles; I'll run and not be weary; I'll walk and not faint.

I've learned to keep my hand in God's hand. You've got to keep your hand in His and your eyes fixed on Him. Don't let anybody turn you around. Don't turn to the left. Don't turn to the right. Don't throw up your hands and don't throw in the towel. Don't turn your back. Don't walk away. And don't shut your eyes. Because in a moment, in the twinkling of an eye, God has a blessing for you. I'm telling you, hold on. I've learned that "Weeping may endure for a night, but joy comes in the morning" (Ps. 30:5).

Joy and Peace

Contentment means I have joy right where I am. The devil may take my money, my friends, my family, but unless I hand it over to him, he can't have my joy. You've got to stand up in the boldness of the Holy Ghost and tell Satan to get his hands off your joy. When you are weak, the joy of the Lord is your strength. I've learned some things. I've been in ditches before. I've been down before. I've been in trouble before too. But I've learned that whatsoever state I am in to be content. I know that if I hold on, God will show up. When He shows up, He'll show out. He'll pick me up and bless me. He'll let me look back at all the stuff He brought me out of or kept me in. Then He'll show me all the things the devil took from me, everything he stole from me. And He'll tell me, "Now, go back and get everything that belongs to you. Go get your marriage, go get that job, go get that child, go get that happiness, and by all means, go get your smile. And praise Me every step of the way!"

When I am content, I'm okay where I am because I know that God is on the way. And there's peace. Not quiet, but peace, the kind that surpasses all understanding. Now, that means two things. First, the folks who look at you don't understand. Some of you have people in your lives right now, and they know what you're going through. They know the trials you're facing, and they don't understand why you still have your joy. You still have your peace of mind. You still have a smile on your face. You've still got your glow. They don't understand that. God has given you peace that the world doesn't understand.

Then God says not only will it pass their understanding, it'll pass all understanding, meaning sometimes you won't understand it yourself. It won't make sense to you. You know that some others who have gone through what you've been through lost their minds a long time ago. But this didn't happen to you. You've got peace. You don't always understand it, but you've got it.

Peace flows from contentment. Unrest is a by-product of discontentment. Discontentment is dangerous. Discontentment will make you put up with stuff that you don't even deserve. Discontentment is bad for your spiritual health. It will silence your prayers. Show me a person who is in bondage to discontentment, and I'll show you a person who doesn't pray.

Contentment is a declaration of my faith. It is thanking God while I am where I am, because I know He'll bring me out in due season. So, if I am poor, I declare I am rich. If I am weak, I declare I am strong.

I'm going to challenge you. I'm going to put you on the spot. God has assigned you to read this book because He knows that, in your heart, you desire to be a godly man or woman. But He also knows that in your heart there is some discontentment. You never knew there was a connection between discontentment and godliness until now. So I challenge you to thank Him now. Thank Him while you're still unemployed or single or broke or depressed. Thank Him while you're still exercising yourself unto godliness. And remember, godliness with contentment is great gain.

Prayer
for
Contentment

Gracious Heavenly Father, I thank You.
I thank You first for the love you showed me in
    giving Your Son to save me.
I thank You for the mercy that did not leave me
    in my sin.
Thank You for the sunshine and the rain.
Father, I want to be content wherever I am.
I ask You to show me the blessing in my
    circumstances. Please open my eyes to see
    Your grace and its sufficiency.
Remind me how You have delivered me and
    protected me.
Show me places in my life where Your hand held
    me when I would have fallen.
Put praises on my lips.
Let my life praise You.
Clothe me with Your glory, that others might
    see You and praise You too.
In Jesus' name, Amen.

Chapter 11 Exercises

Exercise 1: A Lesson in Contentment

1. Memorize Philippians 4:11:

For I have learned in whatever state I am, to be content.

2. Contentment is learned through experience. The fact that it is learned means "it is attainable only with the Holy Spirit, who teaches all things." What things in your life are you learning through experience?

3. Discontent is a symptom of a lack of faith. If you are not content with the way God is doing things, there is something in you that believes there is a better way, even if you don't immediately see it. Are there areas in your life where you are discontent?

Exercise 2: Blessings

Part 1: Blessed?

Think of someone you see as more blessed than you. In what ways are they more blessed?

_____

_____

_____

Now write about someone you see as less blessed.

_____

_____

_____

On a scale of 1–10, how blessed are you in the following areas? Explain.

Personally _____

_____

_____

_____

Financially _____

_____

_____

_____

At Work _____

_____

_____

_____

Spiritually _____

_____

_____

_____

Friendships _____

_____

_____

_____

Physically _____

_____

_____

_____

Romantically _____

_____

_____

_____

Part 2: I Am Blessed!
Now read the following Scriptures and paraphrase them in
the space provided:

Hebrews 13:5

_____

_____

Philippians 4:19

_____

_____

Colossians 3:1–2

_____

_____

Ephesians 1:4–6

_____

_____

Revelation 22:14

_____

_____

Romans 8:29–31

_____

_____

Philippians 1:6

_____

_____

2 Peter 1:2–4

_____

_____

1 Corinthians 10:24

_____

_____

Now, look at the first part of the exercise again. Is your opinion of how blessed you are different from God's view of how blessed you are? If so, take a moment to pray and ask God to bring you closer to His view of your life.

Exercise 3: Discontentment

1. What are your issues of discontent? Tell God. If you have none, tell Him that too.

2. What is the wealth in your life? Listen. Let God tell you. Write. Remember.

3. Pray with your heart. If you're not sure how to start, begin by using the prayer path provided for you (p. 232). Don't forget to say thank you.

Notes

Chapter 2

1. Bradley P. Holt, *A Brief History of Christian Spirituality* (Oxford: Lion Publication, 1993), 12.

2. Eric Carlton, *Patterns of Belief: Peoples and Religion* (London: George Allen & Unwin Ltd., 1973), 18.

3. Philip Sheldrake, *Spirituality and Theology* (London: Darton, Longman, and Todd, Ltd., 1998), 199.

4. Holt, *A Brief History of Christian Spirituality*, 16.

5. Philip Sheldrake, *Spirituality and History* (London: SPCK, 1995), 41.

6. Ibid., 40.

7. Bishop Michael Marshall, article in *The Church of England Newspaper*, 7 August 1998, 17.

8. Sheldrake, *Spirituality and History*, 41.

9. Tony Evans, *What a Way to Live!* (Nashville: Word Publishing, 1997), 5.

10. Michael Downey, *Understanding Christian Spirituality* (New York: Paulist Press, 1997), 8.

11. Evans, *What a Way to Live!*, 88.

12. Ibid., 89.

13. Kenneth Leech, *The Eye of the Storm* (London: Darton, Longman and Todd, Ltd., 1992), 14.

14. Jerry Bridges, *The Pursuit of Holiness* (Colorado Springs: NavPress Publishing Group, 1996), 15.

15. Ibid.

16. John Stott, "The Secret of Holiness" taped sermon, All Souls Cassettes, E42/1b.

17. Rudolf Otto as quoted by J. I. Packer, *Rediscovering Holiness* (Ann Arbor, Mich.: Servant Publications, 1992), 131.

18. Rudolf Otto, *The Idea of the Holy* (London: Oxford University Press, 1950), 12ff.

19. Fritz Rienecker and Cleon Rogers, *A Linguistic Key to the Greek New Testament* (Grand Rapids: Regency Reference Library, 1976), 429.

20. John Stott, *Focus on Christ* (Grand Rapids: Zondervan Publishing House, 1979), 52.

21. Jonathan Edwards, *Religious Affections* (Minneapolis: Bethany House Publishers, 1984), 100.

Chapter 3

1. Authur Bennett, ed., *The Valley of Vision* (Carlisle, Penn.: The Banner of Truth Trust, 1975), 8. Used by permission.

2. John MacArthur, *The John MacArthur Study Bible* (Nashville: Word Publishing, 1997), 1697.

Chapter 8

1. Rienecker and Rogers, *A Linguistic Key to the Greek New Testament*, 518.

Chapter 9

1. Jack Hayford, in a sermon near Mount Zion in Jerusalem, March 1998.

About the Author

*B*ISHOP KENNETH C. ULMER is pastor of the Faithful Central Missionary Baptist Church, a charismatic Baptist congregation located in Los Angeles. His sensitivity to following God's leading has resulted in a rich spiritual and personal legacy.

Dr. Ulmer serves on the Board of Trustees of The King's College and Seminary in Los Angeles, and was one of the founders of the Full Gospel Baptist Church Fellowship, where he was bishop of Christian Education. He was the author of the doctrinal statement of that body and the editor of *The Full Gospel*, its Christian Education curriculum.

Bishop Ulmer holds a Bachelor of Arts in Broadcasting/Music from the University of Illinois, a Master of Arts in Biblical Studies and a Doctor of Philosophy from Grace Graduate School of Theology, a Doctor of Ministry from United Theological Seminary, and an honorary Doctor of Divinity from the Southern California School of Ministry. He is a dynamic teacher who has taught at Biola University, Fuller Theological Seminary, Grace Theological Seminary (West Campus), and Pepperdine University. He frequently conducts seminars and workshops at colleges and universities across the nation, as well as being a regular speaker for Promise Keepers.

Dr. Ulmer and his wife, Togetta, have been married since 1977 and are parents of two daughters, RoShaun and Keniya, and one son, Kendan. The Ulmers reside in Los Angeles.